"Let m̲ ... en-Y employees and wondered ... ̲truggling with find-ing the be̲ ... ̲d them? Then this book is a ̲ ... ̲t only why they act the way th ... and expectations. It also provides great, easy to execute strategies on how to build strong and col-laborative relationships in our time-crunched world. Kudos to Dr. Lipkin and Dr. Perrymore for finally giving us the ultimate user's guide to Gen Y!"
—Stacey C. Cunningham, CEO and chief strategist, SCC & Company

"Boomers and Gen Xers who shake their heads in frustration as they speak of Generation Y will be nodding in appreciation after reading this smart, fair-minded, and extraordinarily readable explanation of what makes our future leaders tick."
—Wes Mann, editor, *Investor's Business Daily*

"Gen-Y employees are quickly becoming a force in the workplace. This outstanding book will help every leader better understand and manage this talented group of employees."
—David F. Jones, management consultant and executive coach, DavidJones Group, LLC and author of *Surviving and Thriving after Losing Your Job*

"In **Y in the Workplace**, Nicole Lipkin and April Perrymore offer practical guidance to help understand the unique challenges posed by the growing number of Gen Y's at work. Although grounded in psychological and motivational theory (as evidenced by the tidbit references they serve 'Shrinkwrapped'), the book is easy to read and replete with practical advice to address Gen-Y behaviors. Savvy manag-ers of earlier generations will read this book and follow the recommended actions. Savvy members of Gen Y will read this book to better understand how they are perceived and, consequently, to adjust their behaviors, capitalizing on their Gen Y strengths and aiming to become highly prized, "low maintenance" employees."
—Joseph E. Sinclair, SPHR, human resources manager, Evonik RohMax USA, Inc.

"Psychologists Perrymore and Lipkin have created wonderful ideas on how to incorporate the members of Gen Y into the corporate world. They offer specific strategies (such as the Ice Cream Sandwich) that will help both managers and Gen Yers to create a shared vision of success."

—M.L. Corbin Sicoli, PhD, professor of psychology, Emerita-Cabrini College

"A majority of my work force fits this demographic to a 'T.' Many of the characteristics described in terms of approach to dress and work behavior is evidenced to me on a daily basis. This book provides wonderful psychological insight to Generation Y but the key pieces were the coaching suggestions based on the theoretic underpinnings. They were easy to pick up and remember and equally easy in application. I have used a few successfully and was amazed at how much easier it was to get some to 'move their needle' using your suggestions. It is clear that Drs. Lipkin and Perrymore are speaking from in-depth experience and understanding of this frequently perplexing group."

—Steven Gilbert, RPh, MBA, BCPS, vice president of operations, PHL Care Center, Hospice Pharmacia

"**Y in the Workplace** is a must-read for managers, presenting a clear-eyed look at the generation now in their 20s. Too many other books focus on unsupported ideas of Gen Y as rule-following conformists, but this book tells the truth businesspeople need to know: that this is a generation of independent thinkers with all of the both bad and good things that go along with that. This is the first book I've seen that discusses the workplace implications of Gen Y's true generational personality, in all of its individualism and desire for work-life balance. Even better, it offers concrete solutions about how to work with Gen Y. Absolutely essential."

—Jean Twenge, author of *Generation Me* and coauthor of *The Narcissism Epidemic*

"As someone who deals with high-powered Gen Y students every day in the classroom, I can only imagine what employers must be up against. But do not despair—help is on the way! Nicole Lipkin and April Perrymore have discovered how to bring out the best of this talented but distracted generation. It turns out that Gen Y employees actually work—but they work differently. Read this book and find out how to coach them to success."

—G. Richard Shell, Thomas Gerrity professor, Wharton School of Business and coauthor of *The Art of Woo*

Y in the Workplace

Managing the "Me First" Generation

By Nicole A. Lipkin and
April J. Perrymore

The Career Press, Inc.
Pompton Plains, NJ

Y in the Workplace
Edited and Typeset by Gina Talucci
Cover design by Ian Shimkoviak, The Book Designers
Printed in the U.S.A.

To order this title, please call toll-free 1-800-CAREER-1 (NJ and Canada: 201-848-0310) to order using VISA or MasterCard, or for further information on books from Career Press.

The Career Press, Inc., 220 West Parkway, Unit 12
Pompton Plains, NJ 07444
www.careerpress.com

Library of Congress Cataloging-in-Publication Data
Lipkin, Nicole A.
   Y in the workplace : managing the "me first" generation / by Nicole A. Lipkin and April J. Perrymore.
         p. cm.
   Includes bibliographical references and index.
   ISBN 978-1-60163-071-1
   1. Supervision of employees. 2. Generation Y. I. Perrymore, April J. II. Title.

HF5549.12.L54 2009
658.3'02--dc22
                                                    2009007683

——Dedication——

To our family and friends, our personal "giants."

-Acknowledgments-

Writing this book has been a life-changing process that would not have been possible without the "shoulders" of our own personal giants. Together we would like to begin by thanking, Michael Snell, our agent, for believing in our idea and turning our dreams of writing this book into a reality. We also would like to thank the Career Press editors and publishers for their support, their dedication, and for making this book possible.

Thank you to our devoted reviewers who took on a non-paying, part-time job without even realizing what they were getting themselves into: Ethan Lipkin, our "Everything Expert and our Gen X Cohort," for being an unending well of information. We appreciate your humor, critical thought, creativity, and ability to challenge us with the other side of every thought. Till Manthey, our "Critical Eye and Gen Y Advocate," for your unique perspectives, grammatical expertise, funny comments, and insightful thoughts. You forced us to challenge our perspectives and ideas. Soryoung Rosa Kim, PsyD, our "Fellow Psychologist and Gen Y Expert," for your compassionate and diplomatic feedback and incredible input. Your insight and wisdom encouraged us to look at all sides comprehensively. Diane Perrymore, our "Human Resource and Business Expert," for your experience, advice, and support. We are especially thankful for your rapid and inspiring responses to our frequent questions and requests. Stacy Cunningham, our "Business and Coaching Expert," for putting us on the right path every time. We see you as our beacon that guided our writing, and this book, in the right direction. And Jennifer Perrymore, our "Business and Marketing Expert," for listening, reading, and commenting on our thoughts and written words with the utmost honesty. We are thankful for the way you think about the world and that you have remarkable ability to see problem areas and offer solutions.

We are thankful for all of our interviewees/business leaders who graciously provided their experiences and stories. We appreciate the time of our library consultant, Ann Schwelm, who quickly found the research for which we were looking. We are grateful to our Generation Y students and clients of the past and present. Your talent and potential constantly amaze us.

A special shout out to Chapter House Café and Gallery, the independent coffee house where we spent more hours than we spent at home. Thank you to the welcoming owners and staff for letting us camp out with an endless source of comfy chairs, coffee, tea, and goodies.

We are appreciative of each other and the synergy we have shared during this process. To write a book with a close friend lends to being able to work and play at the same time. Here's to broken laptops, long hours, all of life's experiences during this writing process, amicable disagreements, warm-hearted conversations, and a beautiful friendship.

Nicole has been honored and humbled by this process and the support and love that she has received. She is deeply appreciative of all of her beautiful and wonderful friends and family who made this process possible by standing by her side, cheering her on, and providing a few laughs along the way (you know who you are). She would especially like to thank her brother and friend, Ethan, not only for his help with this book, but also for being her greatest support and the person who encourages her to chase after her dreams. She would also like to thank two amazing friends, Till and Rosa, not only for their contribution to this book, but also for their unconditional faith and their unending love, support, and encouragement for all of her big ideas. Her two fabulous cats, El Guapo Meatball and Kreplach, also deserve a big thank you, because they still seem to love her even though she was spending more time at the coffee shop, then spending time with them. She would also like to acknowledge the memory of her parents. Without their grace, humor, love, and strength, she would not be the woman she is today.

April would like to thank Paul Perrymore, the love of her life, for his encouragement, endless support for her dreams, making her laugh, and tolerance for the fact that all of her sentences lately have begun with "Gen Y this, Gen Y that." She is extremely grateful to her mom, a BFF, who taught her among many life lessons, the importance of helping others. April is also deeply appreciative of her family and wonderful friends: Paul, Mom, Dad, Glenn, David, Elaine, Kristin, Erin, Little Glenn, Mom II, Dad II, Jen, Keith (wish you were here), Aunt Peg, Traci, Mike, Logan, G. Gasior, Erica, Tricia, Kristen, DJ, and Candi S. It is because of your love and support that she is filled with lightness of heart and spirit that allow the freedom to delve so deeply into her life's work.

Contents

Foreword

Y in the Workplace, by Nicole Lipkin and April Perrymore, is a must-read for anyone who has been puzzled by or frustrated with their Gen Y coworkers. This is a straightforward, tell-it-like-it-is approach to the youngest generation in today's workforce. Through the use of no-brainer, brainer, and big brainer coaching solutions, the authors provide page after page of concrete advice that readers can immediately put into action. Within each chapter, the perspectives of Gen Y's, leaders, and Human Resource representatives are offered, in addition to the keen insights and observations of the authors.

Y in the Workplace challenges the stereotypes of Gen Y that too often get in the way of effective communication. These are replaced with a balanced description of the advantages and drawbacks of working with Gen Y's, based on extensive interviews with Gen Y's, leaders, and HR across several organizations.

The authors established four objectives at the beginning of the book from which readers can gain:

› A good understanding of the strengths and challenges that Generation Y is bringing to the workplace.

› Insight into the psychological underpinnings and the zeitgeist that shapes Generation Y and influences what they bring to the workplace.

› Useful coaching strategies and solutions to effectively transition this generation into the workforce, and to help them develop their strengths and diminish their weaknesses.

› An instillation of hope about Gen Y's abilities to impact the future legacy of companies in an exciting way.

These objectives are more than met! I have a brighter outlook for the future of U.S. organizations because of the authors' sound, practical approach to leveraging Gen Y's skills and talents.

—Linda Gravett
coauthor of *Bridging the Generation Gap*

Preface

We are both psychologists in our 30s, born smack in the middle of our generation, Generation X. Yes, we were that generation that drove you crazy before Generation Y came along. We sat eagerly watching as MTV was born with the premier of the Buggles "Video Killed the Radio Star" and created our first computer program with a ball bouncing across the computer screens of our Apple II's. We excelled at QBert and Pacman on Atari. We embraced rubber bracelets, side ponytails, and fluorescent-colored clothing, and constantly said "as if," "gag me with a spoon," "totally tubular," and "jammin" just like our Gen-X peers. We too grew up thinking our generation was the best, and felt that our parents and grandparents, the Boomers and Veterans, could not understand our angst and our experience. As we entered into our own adulthoods and took on leadership positions, we also found ourselves, as well as our Gen-X and Boomer friends, complaining about the younger generation who appeared so different than our generation. Who are these kids that think the world owes them so much?

As we were writing this book, we realized that we were communicating more via e-mail, text, and IM than having face-to-face meetings. We too multitask like madwomen and are thankful for our iPods and iPhones. We also are both small business owners and decided to pursue entrepreneurship because we value flexibility and freedom in our work. As we were writing this book, we realized that many of the skills, traits, and values espoused by Generation Y as a whole have assimilated positively into our lives and careers.

Preface

The idea for this book came to us as we were discussing the changes we have seen in our careers while working with Generation Y and after hearing similar stories from our intergenerational friends, coworkers, clients, and encounters during "couching" and consulting assignments. As psychologists, professors, consultants, and coaches, we enter the worlds and minds of this generation, as well as other generations, in a unique way. We have heard what they think about and how they approach the world and their careers, and we have developed a deep appreciation for this generation and the challenges and strengths they bring with them wherever they go. We have witnessed that this generation does not like being told what to do, but wants to be told what to do. Makes no sense? Exactly! They also appear to have a sense of entitlement and expect that opportunities will be showered upon them immediately. They are, however, incredibly well-traveled, diverse, accepting, and unbelievably socially and globally conscious.

Ironically, outside of our psychological, coaching, teaching, and consultation experiences, one of our best sources of information was at our local coffee shops and cafés. It is fairly common to hear people complain about their work and their coworkers in these places. We are not chronic eavesdroppers, but as psychologists, we are good listeners and have overheard, over and over again, people from other generations complaining about Generation Y. People are talking about this generation constantly, often complaining about the same things, such as their sense of entitlement, their high expectations, or their inability to accept feedback. The more we listened, in conjunction with our work, interviews, and research, the clearer the behavioral patterns of this generation became. We must note, however, that we wrote the majority of this book in a local coffee shop, mostly filled with unemployed and student Gen Y's. Again, we are not chronic eavesdroppers (really, we're not), but guess what? They are complaining about their older predecessors just as much as the Boomers and Xers are complaining about them. We realized that our somewhat unique perspective derived from working so closely for years with both the Gen Y's and the generations that manage them would lend to writing a book that offers insight into why this generation behaves the way they do, and would prove to be very helpful for those in the position of managing the Gen Y's.

To gather the information for this book, we were fortunate enough to speak with a variety of different Xer and Boomer managers, supervisors, teachers, and professors, who have direct experience either working with and/or hiring and firing Generation Y employees. We were also able to talk with many Gen Y's to get their insights and opinions. Although this generation is made up of those born between 1980 and 2000, we are focusing on those Ys that dominate in the workplace, currently between the ages of 18 and 28 years old. We acknowledge that we make broad generalizations throughout this book and are fully aware that our generalizations do not represent every Gen Yer, just like the broad generalizations made about every previous generation do not reflect each member. In addition, we talk about developmental issues that many Gen Y's have been privy to, such as an emphasis on self-esteem building, overly involved parenting, and unconditional financial and emotional support. However, we concede that not every Gen Yer has had the luxury of prolonged parental support, financial means and security, high-quality educational and extracurricular opportunities, access to technology, and were encouraged to speak openly and freely. Although there are individual differences, and it would be impossible for us to cover how each and every Gen Y behaves in the workforce, we hope to share our insights, guidance, appreciations, frustrations, and laughs about this generation (and yours), so you can help mold them in the necessary areas and appreciate them for who they are and what they can contribute to your company.

───Chapter 1───

Flip-Flops and MySpace: Introduction to Gen Y and the Workplace

> Cody was the valedictorian of his graduating class at Harvard and wears flip-flops to work.

> Kayla is a technological genius with a nose ring and purple-streaked hair.

> Hunter spent two years in the Peace Corps working on human rights issues in Africa and can't stop saying "dude" at formal meetings, including meetings with his clients.

> Ashley was a gymnasticss and soccer star since the age of five, president of her student body, and captain of the drama club, dance club, and debate team, and cannot stop calling her mom at work on her cell phone, IM-ing her friends on her computer, and listening to her iPod while she works on "menial" tasks.

What do all of these bright stars have in common? They are the first generation who got carted around in huge SUVs with "Baby on Board" signs announcing their arrival. They are the first generation of "winners," because they were not allowed or able to lose in school, and basically got gold stars just for showing up. They are the first generation who stopped passing notes in class and started text messaging instead. They are also the first generation that went to elementary school with cell phones in their messenger bags, attended high school with metal detectors, and were entering or leaving college when our world began marching to the tune of a new color: "code orange."

Who are they? They are the Y's. Generation Y that is; otherwise known as the Nexters, Echo Boomers, Internet Generation, iGeneration, Generation Why, and Millennials. Although there is little consensus on the name for the generation born between 1980 and 2000, this 73 to 75 million person generation is close in size to the 78 million Boomers and significantly larger than Gen X (49–50 million). Like the proverbial stampede of bulls in a china shop, Generation Y has stormed the workplace created by the Veterans and Boomers, and is demanding that changes be made to the corporate culture and landscape. Their sheer size as a generation makes their voices as loud and their influence as strong as the Boomers.

This generation is multitalented, over stimulated, socially aware, demanding, and resourceful. They are also utterly challenging and confusing to the global workplace, as well as to their supervisors and managers, who happen to be the same age as their extremely supportive, hovering "helicopter" parents. Most of you Boomers and Xers reading this book annoyed your parents too, with your rebellious nature and respective music preferences. Generation Y is doing the same thing in the workforce: rebelling against pantyhose, pearls, briefcases, and in-person meetings in exchange for nose rings, messenger bags, and instant messaging.

Generation Y was raised on a healthy dose of self-esteem and "you can be anything that you want to be" mentality. Their Boomer and older Gen-X parents rebelled against the more traditional parenting styles of their parents (for example, children are seen but not necessarily heard, children show respect to authority figures no matter what, children work hard to earn reward and recognition). As a consequence of this revolt, parents pressured school systems to change their approach to education, overemphasizing self-esteem, and instilling a system of rewards not based on merit.

This shift is understandable. The threat of global terrorism, bullet wounds in gym class, and even the perceived environmental meltdown of planet Earth makes some re-evaluate what is important in life. Parenting goals for Gen Y centered on having positive, strong relationships with their children, supporting, honoring, and protecting them no matter what, and providing them with every opportunity for growth and expression. This parental revolt coupled with cultural changes that have ensued throughout the past 20 years (academically, socially, politically, environmentally, globally, technologically) have created enormous changes in the upbringing of Generation Y and their subsequent behavior in the workplace. Common Gen Y behaviors that need to be addressed in the workplace include:

› Talking or text messaging on cell phones while working and during meetings.

› Addressing why visible piercings on the face and wearing flip-flops are not suitable business attire.

› Convincing this generation that not everybody gets to make their own hours.

› Helping them understand why they are not going to be able to be in a high-leadership position during their first year of employment.

› Educating them that it is inappropriate to speak with supervisors, managers, and CEOs with the same tone and informality as friends.

› Mending meltdowns when a mistake is made or feedback is given.

Due to their upbringing and the cultural zeitgeist that predominated while they were growing up, this generation has an entirely different work ethic, attitude, and a different set of values shaking the foundation of workplaces everywhere. The frustrations of management from previous generations are clear because they worked hard, sacrificing family time, performing menial tasks to please their supervisors, and working long hours (in some cases at the expense of their health), to earn respect and get promoted. The frustrations of Generation Y are also clear, as they want to live now rather than live when they retire. Generation Y values their free time, energy, and health during long hours at the office and they insist that work be part of life, not life itself. Here in lies the value contrast that is causing tremors throughout corporate America right now. Sure the Y's have their drawbacks; however, hasn't every generation said that about every other generation?

Every generation has a touch of generational centrism, or what we term "gencentrism," the belief that their generation is the most unique, advanced, and capable, as compared to all preceding generations. In turn, every generation has complained about the inadequacies of the generation before and after them. However, every generation influences the next generation and that generation influences the next and so on. So the Boomers and older Xers, the parents of the Y's, have developed and nurtured the characteristics and traits of this generation who are driving many of them crazy. The truth is, every generation has had members of their generation that have made things more difficult for everyone else, and every generation has had their amazing, talented members who have made the world a better place. The same holds true for Generation Y. There will be some Gen Y's who, like the 9 to 5, are happy to wear a suit, and have no qualms about working their way up the corporate ladder. Others, well…not so much. Throughout our coaching, consulting, and research, we learned that many of the same workplace issues with regard to the Y's came up over and over again. So for the purposes of this book "some members of" and/or "a segment of," when we refer to Generation Y (Y's, Yers, and so on), we are referring to the applicable members of the generation.

Y in the Workplace

As a whole, this generation is a group of "catapultors." More specifically, they can either catapult to the top of your organization and illuminate your company's potential with their talents, or they can catapult right out of your organization into the hands of your competitors. As you have learned through your experiences and what you will learn from this book, the Veteren/Boomer phenomenon of loyalty to a company is not a value espoused by this generation. Therefore, to attract, retain, engage, and groom Generation Y for success in leadership, contribution, and their ability to honor the legacy you will leave, we suggest taking a step back and developing a true understanding of this generation and why they are the way they are.

After speaking with Boomer and Xer managers and supervisors for this book, what we realized is that some of you are excited by the infiltration of the Ys into the workplace, but the majority of you are frustrated, concerned, and standing there with mouths agape at the audacity of some of your younger employees. Some of you have expressed concerns that the negative characteristics of this generation as a whole are less a function of age and maturity, but rather manifest in their ability to sustain a system of workplace values that have the potential to create a huge negative impact on the work environment. Concerns regarding succession planning and leaving a positive legacy within the hands of this generation have been expressed with the feeling that the task will be frustrating and fruitless because of the perceived arrogance and entitlement with which this generation operates. Some of you have also expressed your anger and resentment about changing how you operate and feeling that the culture of your workplace will change because of this generation.

We suggest taking a step back, taking a deep breath, and re-evaluating your current generational conundrum. This generation, just like your generation and every generation that has come before, has brought with them specific challenges, as well as wonderful opportunities and talents to the workplace. This generation is and will continue to be no different. You do not have to revamp your workplace values or approach to successfully incorporate this generation into the workplace. Rather, we recommend being open-minded by truly hearing what they have to say and contribute, so that you can groom them successfully and effectively. There is a happy medium between your values and ways of operating, and their values and way of operating. You do not have to change yourself for them; however, you may need to adapt some policies in order to extract the benefits from this new generation of employees.

In order to get to that middle ground, preconceived notions and stereotypes need to be put aside, so that progress can actually be made. Again, this generation has not only been influenced by the political, environmental, and social culture in which they were raised, they were also influenced by you. As their managers, you have the largest influence on how this generation will continue to work and impact corporations and businesses in the future. To truly get your minds going in the right direction, reflect on the following questions:

> › Think about a few of your Gen Y employees. What adjectives would you use to describe them?

> › What bothers you most about your Gen Y employees?

> › What most impresses you about your Gen Y employee?

Keep these questions in mind as you read this book. It will help you individualize your experience and tailor your coaching strategies and plans to help your younger employees become successful contributors and leaders in your organizations.

"Shrink" those Gen Y's

How? Well, because we are psychologists, we took a different approach to writing this book about Generation Y than some of the other books out on the market. We wrote this book with the intention of providing some psychological insight into why this generation behaves the way they do, rather than just identifying the problems. We also offer techniques for working within your Gen Y's current modus operandi and molding them to be more supervisor and organizationally friendly.

We see this generation as a strong generation with an incredible amount of potential and vast array of strengths to offer the workplace. Rather than simply outlining the strengths and challenges, we have pulled from our experience and training as psychologists, professors, and consultants to explain the psychological, cultural, social, and environmental reasons why this generation presents the way it does. When insight into the behavior of others is gained the development of a deeper appreciation or empathy often occurs. With this empathy and knowledge at the forefront, you are less likely to give up and more likely to want to understand where someone is coming from. We are providing you with the tools to develop unique insight into the functioning of this generation, so you can be more informed, less frustrated, and groom them in a way that develops their skills by harnessing their strengths and minimizing their weaknesses.

Ready to read? Here's what you need to know first

Each chapter focuses on important areas of development or environmental influences that have directly impacted the workplace. Although generalizations about Gen Y's behaviors, attitudes, and workplace impacts are made throughout this book, keep in mind that these generalizations are not representative of every member of Gen Y. Also, to protect the identities of some Gen Y's and their managers, several names have been changed. Although we tried our best to order the chapters in a way that continually builds on increasing your understanding and knowledge of Gen Y, if you have a particular problem area (for example, wanting to know how to manage a Gen Y who is constantly seeking your reassurance and feedback), by all means jump to that chapter (Chapter 4) to get the information you need. Each chapter consists of the following:

> **Psychological basics:** Insight into the psychological, social, cultural, and environmental reasons why this generation presents the way they do with regard to the topic at hand.

> **How it plays out in the workplace:** The influence of specific strengths and challenges in the workplace based on observation, experience, and stories we have heard from managers and supervisors.

> **Coaching solutions:** Targeted strategies and solutions to harness this generation's strengths and minimize their weaknesses within the area being addressed. Effective coaching strategies are described with evidence of why it works. Coaching solutions are varied in their level of difficulty:

   ▪ **No Brainers:** strategies and solutions that can be put in place immediately with little effort.

   ▪ **Brainers:** strategies and solutions that require a bit more time and effort.

   ▪ **Big Brainers:** strategies and solutions that require an organizational shift to incorporate and may take more time to implement.

Throughout the book, there are special features highlighting stories, suggestions, and tips. Special features include:

> **Shrinkwrapped:** Provides further explanation of psychological concepts introduced throughout the book. These tidbits help you think like a shrink.

› **Did this really happen? Yes!:** Stories that we gathered from managers and supervisors that made us shake our heads in disbelief, feel appalled, and sometimes even laugh out loud.

› **A leader says:** Tips, stories, and comments offered by managers and supervisors.

› **HR chimes in:** Tips, stories, and comments from human-resource professionals.

› **A Gen Y says:** Opinions and comments gathered from Generation Y individuals.

We will also refer to different technology, digital media, communication formats, and terms that are second nature to Gen Y. Here's a little guide to keep in mind when reading this book or when working with your Gen Y employees:

› **Twitting**—The act of twitting occurs when you type a comment on Twitter, a free social networking and micro-blogging Website, where you can post and read other users' updates (which are known as "tweets").

› **IMing**—Instant messages that are typed and sent through the Internet.

› **Gchat**—A form of IMing for those who use Gmail (Google's e-mail).

› **Texting**—The term for a short message sent to a cell phone.

› **Friendster**—Known as the first social networking site popular with teenagers and those in their 20s. Currently more popular in other countries than it is in the United States.

› **Facebook**—A social networking Website that connects people with their friends where they can post comments, exchange information, and pictures for their friends to see. Facebook offers the ability to search for names and send e-mails requesting to be friends with those you search for (for example, attended the same school, worked at the same company, lived in the same geographical area). There is also a feature on Facebook that allows users to post updates of what they are currently doing or thinking at any moment of the day or night.

› **FriendFeed**—A social sharing site that allows people to keep informed about different videos, photos, Web pages, and music that their friends are sharing.

› **Digg**—An online, user-rated tool for people to share and rate content that is on the Web.

> **MySpace**—A social networking Website for anyone over the age of 14. Personal information, blogs, and photos can be posted. You can invite friends to your list and send them private messages, posted messages, personal information, and blogs. It can be seen by anyone that has a MySpace account.

> **LinkedIn**—A professional networking site used to reconnect/connect with past and present colleagues and classmates, discover new business opportunities, and post questions for industry experts.

> **Blogging**—A combination of the word "web" and "log" that describes an online journal which can be shared with others. New entries are placed within the order that they are written about one's experiences and innermost thoughts.

> **YouTube**—A video sharing Website where videos can be uploaded and viewed, and links to share the videos can be e-mailed to others.

> **Message Boards**—An Internet discussion board where thoughts and ideas can be posted and comments can be made to others' postings.

By the last page of this book you will have the perfect Gen Y employee that you have molded into exactly who you want them to be. Okay, maybe not, but we do hope that you will gain the following:

> A good understanding of the strengths and challenges that Generation Y is bringing to the workplace.

> Insight into the psychological underpinnings and the zeitgeist that shapes Generation Y and influences what they bring to the workplace.

> Useful coaching strategies and solutions to effectively transition this generation into the workforce, and to help them develop their strengths and diminish their weaknesses.

> An instillation of hope about Gen Y's abilities to impact the future legacy of companies in an exciting way.

—— Chapter 2 ——

It's All About Me (Okay, and You, Too): Self-Esteem and Generation Y

I deserve good things. I am entitled to my share of happiness. I refuse to beat myself up. I am an attractive person. I am fun to be with...and gosh darn it, people like me!

—Al Franken as Stuart Smalley on *Saturday Night Live*

> "As a Gen Yer and new college graduate, Jacqueline fits all of the stereotypes of this generation that I've heard and read about. On her second day, she let me know that she was expecting to be promoted to a manager position in two to three months, as soon as she showed she 'got' the job. Please note, she has no prior marketing or public relations experience and did not major in either one in college. About two weeks into her employment, she announced that she could not wait until the company hired her staff so that she could sit back and do her nails. I have 15 years of experience in this field. When I have tried to share my experience and give her advice, she let me know in a round-about way that she knew more and didn't need my help. I have been working with her for two months. It has been two months too long. While I am trying to keep in mind that not all Gen Yers are the same as Jacqueline, it is so easy to read an article about Millennials and see where and why they have developed the reputation that they have in the marketplace."
>
> Erica Lui, consultant,
> PR and Marketing

Generation Y has been raised on a large dose of self-esteem, as they have been told that they can be and do anything they want no matter what, which has subsequently produced a population that is self-aware and cognizant of their strengths. Talk to most Gen Y's and they will be able to tell you what they want (grand things) and when they want it (now), but rarely will you hear a realistic, practical plan for how. These big plans and expectations, without the skills or experience to back it up, have been a direct consequence of a generational movement encouraging self-esteem and confidence through upbringing (parenting and education) by their Boomer and Gen X parents. The movement started out with good intentions to support an appropriate development of self-esteem, a quality that is directly related to personal and professional health and success. However, messages of "you can be anything you want to be" and "you are a winner" were provided without the benefits of life experience, and a foundation of real and earned successes, humility, and ability to learn from mistakes. Therefore, as Generation Y has entered the workplace, this "self-esteem movement" has shown its limitations. There are significant consequences of having an exaggerated sense of self-esteem that are directly impacting the workplace today and frustrating managers across the globe. These issues and the impact on the workplace will be explored in detail resulting in concrete solutions and recommendations to assist other generations in helping Generation Y develop a more balanced and workplace-friendly sense of self-esteem.

Back to the (psychological) basics

The basics of self-esteem

Self-esteem, or self-concept, refers to how we think and feel about ourselves in the world. If we have healthy self-esteem then we feel that we are valued, competent, understood, worthy, appreciated, and content with our abilities. People with good self-esteem also tend to be more productive in the workplace and have more mental availability to be creative thinkers. If someone has low self-esteem, they often feel unloved, unworthy, misunderstood, and incompetent. People with low self-esteem may go to great lengths to hide their weaknesses and may often feel wounded if given feedback about areas that need improvement.

It is important to understand the difference between healthy and fragile self-esteem, because this generation has been raised in a way that makes it difficult to figure out what is really going on in the workplace when they display certain behaviors. (For example, unrealistic expectations, cannot take feedback, blaming others for their mistakes, and difficulty with perspective taking). More specifically, the educational system and parenting shifted with this generation more than ever before to focus a great deal on self-esteem building, unintentionally creating what we call the "self-inflation movement." Because Generation Y was the beneficiary of the self-inflation movement as children, and has become the new generation of workers today, the influence of this movement is important to understand because of the tremendous impact it is having on the workplace today.

The self-inflation movement

The self-inflation movement is a direct consequence of the good intentioned self-esteem movement. Raising children to feel good about themselves and encouraging schools to continue supporting this is important. However, along the way, it was demanded (mostly by parents) that accolades for mediocre or failed performance be provided. The self-inflation movement has included:

› Inflated experiences of self-esteem when one performs at subpar levels (for example, awards for getting 10th place).

› Stunted experiences of positive self-esteem that comes naturally when one excels and performs well (because if everyone is getting an award, first place does not hold that same meaning).

› Confidence that they can do and be anything that they want, without the development of realistic, practical, and grounded expectations.

› Protection from any form of failure and blame because blame is often immediately redirected (by parents) onto teachers, coaches, or peers.

This resulted in a generation that can do no wrong. The life experiences of learning from your mistakes, taking ownership for your performance, and developing essential skills when facing challenges were depleted in this self-inflation movement. This movement is so pervasive that even nursery rhymes created during Generation Y's childhoods have also had a focus on the self. For example, one nursery rhyme that infused the preschools and playrooms of your Gen Y employees was called "I'm Glad I'm Me," a nursery rhyme about how great, special, and unique one is in everything they do. Sure, we have come quite a long way from the nursery rhymes of yesteryear with messages of the bubonic plague (ring around the rosy), beheadings (Jack and Jill), and war weaponry (humpty dumpty), but during the childhoods of Gen Yers, it's all about "ME," how great "I" am, how talented "I" am, and how everyone should pay attention to "ME!" Yes, we could argue this sends a better message than a song about execution and pillage (Mary Mary Quite Contrary); however, one could also argue that this type of teaching is creating the execution and pillage of humbleness and self-awareness, two aspects imperative to the development of healthy and adaptive self-esteem.

The roots of the self-inflation movement: parenting

The Boomers were raised at a time where mom stayed home and raised the kids and dad went to work. Social advancements and economic changes that caused both parents to work produced a huge shift during the childhoods of Generation X, the children of the older Boomers, creating the "latchkey kids." Due to the impact and the unforeseen consequences associated with being a latchkey kid (for example, loneliness, academic problems, accidental injury, and impairment of parent-child relationship), the Xers and Boomers who have been raising the Y's have demanded a child-centered approach to child rearing. The environment has responded to these demands, hence the sudden increase of baby gyms and "mommy and me" activities. Also popping up for the first time were the bumper stickers boasting with parental pride and support about honor students ("My kid is an honor student at such-and-such school") and bullies alike ("My kid can beat up your honor student").

Gen Y grew up with the parental message of "My child is right no matter what...even if he/she is really wrong." Then, through time, instead of learning from their mistakes, they were conditioned to stand behind their mother or father thinking, "I am the victim here and mom and dad will make it better." This type of child rearing excludes the important lesson of accepting responsibility for actions. When raised to be a victim, learning from experience, being able to see other points of view, and having a shared reality of events and situations does not occur. When held accountable for your behaviors you develop an understanding of cause and effect, social respect, and experience enhanced self-esteem. When you are able to take ownership of your behaviors, you learn, develop, and grow from the experience. With regard to the workplace, this is a quality that is imperative in the development of positive leadership skills and healthy self-esteem.

This victim mentality and lack of ownership for one's behaviors is best explained in the interview we had with a public school teacher who has felt stifled by the self-inflation movement. She had attempted to interact with parents while teaching this generation self-respect and appropriate self-esteem, which results from taking responsibility and accountability for performance:

> *"I have been teaching children and working with their parents for the past 25 years and have certainly seen quite a change with this generation with regard to self esteem and the impact that parents have had on their children's abilities to develop responsibility and adaptive esteem. There have always been your great, middle of the road, and non-existent parents, and that has not changed in the diverse classrooms that I have taught. However, what has changed is that the parent used to be on the teacher's side. What I mean by that is that teachers and parents worked together more as a team. Now, I feel that I have to continuously calm parents down who think that the reason their child did not succeed was because I did not teach them correctly. When did we stop putting the responsibility on the student and begin placing it on everyone and everything else but the child?"*
>
> *Mrs. Beverly, fifth grade school teacher,*
> *Pennsylvania Public School System*

The roots of the self-inflation movement: education

As a society, we have gone to great lengths to be certain that self-esteem is an important part of our educational system and child-rearing philosophies. The emphasis placed on self-esteem is warranted, but the genuineness of gaining real-life experiences that build self-esteem has been lost. When everyone gets a gold star for basic expectations, such as showing up for school that day, the argument that the self-esteem movement is based on real-life accomplishment is tentative, to say the least. Another story provided to us by a school teacher demonstrates the real-life application of this point:

> *"What's wrong with a curriculum emphasis on self-confidence and self-esteem? Well, I've seen a lot of changes in my 40-plus years as a teacher. One big change was finding games where everyone could be a winner and where no one was eliminated. Games that were played had to be team games. I used to play a beanbag game that the kids loved. There was one winner and*

that winner had the beanbag trophy on their desk for the day. The kids loved it, but because it was an elimination, non-team, only-one-winner game we had to stop playing it. I could see how you would want kids to have success, but it got a little ridiculous. We also had an awards night called 'Recognition Night.' Once the emphasis on self-confidence became a mainstay, we had to find something positive about each child, so that everyone would get an award. Sounds good, but the result was that it lessened those who excelled. It used to be that each child would excel in different ways, but as time went on every child had to be treated the same with no one excelling because everyone won. It used to be that each kid would experience a little bit of failure, but there is no experience of failure within the school curriculum anymore. I think this really hurt our gifted and talented kids, because everyone succeeding has resulted in everyone being mediocre and no one being able to shine."

Mrs. Price, retired third grade school teacher,
New Jersey Public School System

Competition is healthy and provides an environment for learning how to relate and interact with others, as well as how to manage challenges—all of which are critical in the work place. However, due to the self-inflation movement schools and parents demanded less competition in academia and demanded a greater focus on preoccupation with the self. Self-value has been taught through self-focused projects such as "all about me" reports. The development of positive self-feelings were cultivated through unearned trophies, as well as celebrations for behaviors that in the past were just expected rather than rewarded (such as saying please or thank you, treating someone nicely at school, sharing, and studying). Additionally, not failing children who deserved failing grades also enhanced the movement. The expectation of excellence in everything that one does whether it is in school or in afterschool activities, sets children up for difficulty accepting failure and difficulty coping when a mistake is made.

Did this really happen? Yes!

"We have instituted a math challenge program in our school to help increase the math fluency of our students. When a child passes, we reward their success with a certificate that is presented in the cafeteria during lunchtime. All the children get to cheer for their peers when they win a certificate. Since we instituted this program, the percentage of students passing has risen from 35 to 85 percent, and students are really motivated to study their math at

home. The problem is that there have been several parents who have done everything within their power to get the program removed from the school, because these parents say that their children's self-esteem is being hurt when they don't receive a certificate. We've even instituted progress certificates for students who have made good progress toward passing, but still these parents are not satisfied. One parent even wanted us to give her child a certificate saying she passed when she really didn't. This is one of the only things in our school that is a concrete accomplishment that you actually have to earn, which can build a child's self-esteem when they work hard for it and earn it. What the parent doesn't understand is that a certificate without the hard work behind it will be meaningless in the long run. What the parents should be doing is helping the child practice and study, so their child can be successful."

Mrs. Todd, elementary school teacher,
Massachusetts Public School System

Unfortunately, there have been significant side effects to the reduction of competition, rewards regardless of merit, and high expectations of excellence for Generation Y, especially in the workplace. Some of the consequences include:

> Difficulty failing.
> Difficulty tolerating, managing, and learning from their mistakes.
> Poor ability to accept feedback and constructive criticism.
> Trouble using a realistic measuring stick when it comes to self-evaluation of their performance and expectations.
> Blaming others or taking the victim role when mistakes happen.
> Difficulty seeing other perspectives that are not their own.
> Lack of self-awareness.
> Difficulty recognizing their limitations.
> Difficulty taking ownership for decisions and actions.
> Inability to focus on the now.

When Gen Y did make mistakes, blame was placed on others. For example, "Honey, it's not your fault that you failed the spelling quiz, clearly your teacher did not help you learn the words that you needed to learn. Don't worry, I'll call her." This characteristic can carry into adulthood and the workplace. The following story sums up this point perfectly:

> *"I had to give a Gen Y employee feedback about her performance, which was subpar. I knew this was going to be difficult and I had to strategize, so I actually sat down with my HR person to bounce ideas off of her in terms of how I could relay the information, provide recommendations for improvement, and ultimately avoid the scene of her breaking down. At any other time (or with any other generation) I would have stated the facts, offered recommendations about how to improve, and told them that I had confidence in their abilities to make the changes. Well, when I sat down with her and told her my concerns, she immediately burst into tears and told me that it wasn't her fault, but rather my fault for being too stern and her peers' fault for not giving her the information she needed (even though all the information is located on our company intranet). There was absolutely no accountability or responsibility on the employee's part. In fact, I find that this is pretty common with this generation. A lot of these folks have a tough time being corrected and an even tougher time not blaming everyone else for their mistakes."*
> Kevin Mercuri, president
> Propheta Communications

How it plays out in the workplace: advantages of the self-inflation movement

My experience with this generation is that they don't know that anything is impossible. Their lack of experience coupled with their tremendous confidence is an asset.
—Scott Dodson, COO of Divide By Zero Games, Inc.

I can do this, that, and the other thing

Having a healthy dose of self-esteem allows for a healthy dose of self-confidence. Although this confidence is not reflected in every aspect of a Gen Y employee (that is, some display a continuous need for reward and feedback), it is reflected in a sense of confidence of being able to accomplish most tasks assigned to them and the perceived ability to handle different jobs and positions just as well, if not better than the next person (even if that person has 20 years experience on them). This self-assurance also reflects wanting more responsibility although it is often before they accomplish the tasks and responsibilities that are in their job descriptions. When a Gen Y employee enters a company, they expect a promotion quickly and sometimes unrealistically. Although these expectations can be annoying to everyone around, they might also serve as a drive to be successful, and to work hard.

Did this really happen? Yes!

"I was looking to hire someone for the Director of HR position in my company, and I was surprised when one of my new staff members, Melanie, who is in her early 20s and new to the field of HR, applied for the position. Melanie is a wonderful employee, hard working, and very motivated. When she applied for the position, even though she clearly was not ready for that kind of role, I interviewed her for good form. She presented herself well, and interviewed well but was upset when I told her that this position required more work experience in the HR field, and that she should continue to work hard and perhaps apply for the director position in a few years. Although she was upset, I was really impressed with her confidence and initiative in trying for the position and recognized that this type of confidence was truly a characteristic of her generation, as it's not something that I would have ever thought of trying for when I was her age."

Felicia Smith, VP of human resources,
Large Medical Equipment Company

People have always been interested in what I have to say

In comparison to other generations, Gen Y tends to be the most outspoken and bold generation. Their opinions mattered in school and at home, and now they matter in the workplace (whether their managers think so or not). This outspoken/bold quality translates into always having knowledge about what they are thinking, and how they believe that they can contribute to the conversation, to the project, or to the company. They are not afraid to take on challenges, speak up when they have an idea, and make the ball roll when it is placed in front of them. Their confident, outspoken nature coupled with their beliefs of self-importance makes them more apt to take risks and speak up when they have an idea.

A leader says:

"I am a Boomer who started an Internet business a year ago. My business is a boutique music Website that targets the 25 through Boomer age group. I have three Gen Y interns between the ages of 20 and 23 who work with me. My experience is that they are wonderful to work with for two main reasons: one, they are 'yes' people—positive, optimistic, and can-doers. No matter what I ask for, they'll give it a go. The second reason I love working with them is that they are simple—not a lot of clutter, not a lot of paper, not a lot of baggage. They come with their computer and a note pad and that's it. They make simple lists, and check off the projects one by one. Granted, I've hired smart kids, but I think these are traits of their generation as a whole. I'm not sure if it's the age difference, or personality difference but they make my life easier because they get the job done, do it efficiently, they think outside the box, and they give me valuable advice from their point of view. With an Internet business and music Website, I'm learning quickly from them the important skills of their world—keeping things simple and to the point."

Val Haller, owner,
ValsList.com

Oh, I'll try it, it's not like I'm going to fail

The fear of consequences from mistakes, especially in the workplace, that other generations often agonize over prevents, the type of risk taking and going out on a limb that Gen Y engages in naturally. They do not have the same fear because society has taught them not to. Having an extraordinary amount of confidence (whether it is inflated or not), means that one may be more likely to take extraordinary risks. Although risky behaviors are rarely beneficial to a company, the biggest discoveries have often resulted from those that jumped in blindly. The blunt, outspoken, risk-taking nature of Gen Y stems from being able to say anything, at any time, and to be listened to and to receive accolades for original (or not so original) thought.

> **A leader says:**
>
> *"Our 23-year old daughter asked me and my husband if she could work for us after she graduated from college. We own a film and video production company in the San Francisco area and she had been working at a nearby winery, presumably to 'work up the ranks.' It's definitely a big decision when you are operating a Mom-and-Pop shop to hire a kid, let alone your own daughter, when a family business was not in the master plan. Since we made the decision to hire her she has initiated a few very positive projects that warrant mention. At her urging we became the first certified 'green' film and video production company in Marin County. It's been a tremendous PR jolt and we've saved hard dollars due to our environmentally conscious practices. She suggested we produce a documentary on the California wine industry, and this movie,* A State of Vine, *has received great response. As a matter of fact, due to her fast and fluid research capabilities on the Internet, she landed an international distributor for the film, which will be seen on 80 different airlines in the months ahead."*
>
> Christine Scioli, partner,
>
> Zan Media

How it plays out in the workplace: challenges of the self-inflation movement

"Everyone rises to their level of incompetence."
—Laurence J. Peter (1919–1988), "The Peter Principle"

Growing up winners where failure is never an option

Growing up winners, without the option or experience of failure, results in a huge disadvantage in the workforce. We know that mistakes and failures happen in all areas of life. Although these mistakes and failures can be devastating at times, they also serve as important lessons, building blocks in the development of coping mechanisms, learning tools to enhance the self, and they provide opportunities to learn how to accept feedback and constructive criticism. Due to the self-inflation movement pivotal to this generation's developmental experience, they have not been afforded the opportunity to develop appropriate coping skills related to failing or making mistakes. When you cannot make a mistake or fail, you cannot learn from the mistake or failure, therefore you can't recover by developing a new set of skills, coping mechanisms, and underlying lesson learned. This means that when a Gen Y fails or makes a mistake in the workplace, their reaction will have a more dramatic impact than expected, often leaving managers and the bearers of the "you made a mistake" news in shock and disbelief. Of course the saying "we all learn from mistakes" is cliché, but more than ever, it is true. As seen in the following box, ask a seasoned manager working with Gen Y employees and you may hear a story like this.

Did this really happen? Yes!

"I own a promotion company and hire Gen Y employees, mostly because I'm a start-up and can't afford to hire people who have been in the field for a long time. However, all my Generation Y employees want is for me to say, 'Good job, great work, you're amazing,' whether or not they actually did a good job. The bottom line is this generation cannot admit wrongdoing. They get very defensive and threatened and turn it around on you. They can't take ownership of their mistakes. For example, I had one employee to whom I gave a lot of responsibility because she convinced me that she could handle it. I had her run her own promotions event for an important client of mine. She never asked for help planning the event throughout the course of the planning and execution. I showed up at the event with pretty high expectations. However, when I showed up, it was me, her, the client, and that was it. No one else showed up! When I asked her what happened, she said, 'Well, I gave the invitation to the mail house and they were supposed to mail it out.' I asked her if she ever followed up with the mail house and she responded, 'No, why? They were supposed to send it out.' She evidently didn't realize that her job as project manager of the assignment included managing the RSVP process. When I asked her why she didn't ask for help or guidance she said, 'Because I could do it myself. It's not my fault that the mail house screwed up.' Obviously my client was upset because she put all this money up for the event and we ended up losing the account. However, my employee literally could not accept blame for her screw up or analyze her mistakes. In fact, she literally didn't understand that she made a mistake. She would not own up to it at all and kept blaming the mail house for the failed event."

Claudia Ross, owner,

Cross Marketing

Forget the now, I'm onto the next

Another downfall of the self-inflation movement and Gen Y's performance in the workplace is their tendency to be so focused on what's next for them (and the expectation that whatever is next is bigger and better) that they tend to miss the importance of now. This stems from a lack of self-awareness, which often helps keep people grounded and secure in where they are in the moment. This can be incredibly difficult for managers when working to help their Gen Y's develop in the areas where they need assistance. If they are already on to the next step, or their expectation of the next step, then their attention and insight are not present. This becomes a serious problem with regard to grooming your Gen Y employees for leadership positions and has been one of the biggest complaints from professionals we have spoken with. More specifically, developing leadership skills requires being able to stay in the "now" and practice, reflect, and work through your developmental growth areas while honing in on your strengths. Managers we have spoken with have expressed frustration over the difficulty getting their Gen Y employees to even hear the feedback they have to offer, let alone sit and reflect on a developmental issue and problem-solve to get through it.

Shrinkwrapped

Good leaders are able to stay focused on a task, are accountable, are able to see things from other perspectives, are open to constantly improving upon themselves, and are receptive to feedback, even when the feedback is difficult to hear.

If they are not in leadership positions already, Generation Y will undoubtedly be in leadership positions in the near future. Their inflated sense of self coupled with their difficulty of staying in the "now," especially when being provided with coaching and grooming from older colleagues, is reducing their ability to grow and learn through lessons that people with more experience, can provide. We feel that this is one of the biggest drawbacks to the self-inflation movement and can have the greatest negative impact on the work environment.

I can dish it out, but I can't take it

If all you hear is that you are special and you are right no matter what, it is difficult to accurately see the impact you have on other people. It prevents the lack of responsibility taking and blaming others for one's mistakes. We have heard from many managers who report difficulty in getting their Generation Y employees to see their behaviors, performance, and attitudes accurately and to incorporate, much less tolerate, constructive criticism. Raising self-esteem at all costs has resulted in a reinforcement that fault does not lie within, but rather lies outside of the self. Further, it has created difficulty with this generation's ability to regulate themselves independently and to learn from mistakes.

Admitting a mistake is difficult for most people, as it takes self-awareness and engaging in behaviors that strive toward self-actualization. In addition, blaming everyone else for mistakes you have made rather than choosing to own or admit them makes it difficult to accept feedback and criticism for the purposes of growth and development. Overall, in the workplace, being able to see different perspectives on an issue, having insight into how your behaviors impact others, and being able to own your mistakes is imperative and promotes a healthy work environment. Additionally, this helps your Gen Y employees develop positive leadership qualities.

A leader says:

"Because they are the coddled and shielded generation and have been kept from learning from their mistakes, they are really limited in their ability to accept responsibility and take accountability for their actions. Every single Gen Y employee that has gone through my company has cried. The conversation usually begins with, 'I'm disappointed with you,' and the faucet immediately turns on before I can say anything else."

Kent Lewis, president,
Anvil Media, Inc.

The takeaways so far...

If you remember nothing else, takeaway the following:

› There is a thin line between inflated self-esteem and healthy self-esteem, and it is important to understand the difference because of the impact one's self-esteem can have in the workplace with regard to productivity, relationship building, and general workplace functioning.

> Gen Y's upbringing, as influenced by changes in parenting and education, has resulted in an increase in self-focus, lack of responsibility taking, and unrealistic expectations, which is impacting the workplace.

> Inflated self-esteem has resulted in the following behaviors in the workplace: difficulty accepting constructive criticism, inability to tolerate mistakes without blaming others, poor perspective taking, lack of self-awareness, lack of awareness regarding limitations, difficulty taking ownership for decisions and actions, and inability to focus on the now.

> You can use Gen Y's tendency to be self-inflated to your advantage by:

  - Giving them different opportunities and projects to work on outside of their immediate scope of expertise. Their confidence and motivation to excel will surprise you.

  - Listening to their opinions (warranted and unwarranted).

  - Considering the risks that they want to take, even if it appears ridiculous. This is a generation that jumps in with out fear and this has resulted in unexpected success for many Gen Yers and their companies.

> Watch out for Gen Y's tendency to:

  - Have difficulty accepting constructive criticism and feedback.

  - Want to look ahead at the future, rather than staying focused on the "now."

  - Avoid taking responsibility and accountability for their mistakes or weaknesses.

Now it's time to take some action. Here are the coaching solutions that we recommend to enhance the positives and manage the negatives when it comes to the challenges with Generation Y's self-esteem.

Coaching solutions: building on strengths, addressing the challenges

Clearly the way this generation has been raised with regard to their own self worth and esteem has created significant challenges and opportunities for the workplace. Rather than throwing up your hands in frustration, try some of our coaching solutions designed to create opportunities and enhance the positive qualities inherent in a confident, energized, "I can be anything I want to be" employee, and minimize the negative qualities that may be present in your Gen Y employees.

No-brainer coaching solutions

CS1: Turning the "I am, I did, I want" into "tell me more about you" conversation

This coaching solution can be used on an individual basis, as a group exercise or as a team building exercise. It is most beneficial to use with new hires. When using this solution with new hires, we suggest scheduling an hour-long lunch with your new Gen Y employee. Explain that the purpose of this working lunch is to get to know one another, on a personal level, and to be able to hear what the other person is saying without interjecting and changing the topic. This is harder than one would expect, because it requires a skill called "active listening," a skill that is imperative in good leadership development and in life.

Shrinkwrapped

The concept of active listening stems from the therapy work of Carl Rogers. Active listening is the art of being able to suspend judgment and preconceived notions while listening to someone in order to truly hear what is being said. Without responding back with your thoughts and own agenda, it requires you to reflect and summarize what someone has told you by listening with focus. Active listening facilitates genuine positive feelings, a closer relationship, and increased trust.

1. *Stop all other things you are working on to focus on the person speaking.*
2. *Listen without judgment.*
3. *Listen not only to what is being said but also pay attention to the emotion and non-verbal behaviors behind the speaker's words.*
4. *Restate, summarize, or paraphrase what the person has said and ask questions that clarify.*
5. *Be aware of your own thoughts and emotions and only state your views after you have listened to what the other person has said.*

It's All About Me

The exercise requires that one person ask questions while the other person soaks up the information, and at the end explains back to that person what they heard and understood. The time should be equally split between the new hire and the supervisor/manager, and the purpose of the lunch needs to be made clear at the beginning. The following is a list of sample questions that can be used. However, it is recommended that each person come up with five of their own unique questions, based on who they are meeting with and what they want to know about them. Remember this is chance to get to know people personally so the questions should be personal, but not intrusive.

1. How did you get interested in the work you are doing?
2. What was your first job experience?
3. What in life makes you most happy and why?
4. Tell me about your favorite family member.
5. Who is your hero?*
6. What movie or book has most moved you and why?
7. Think of one of your friends and tell me how they would describe you (something great and something not so great).
8. What's something you can tell me about yourself that most people at work would not know?
9. What is the most difficult obstacle you have had to overcome in your life and how did you do it?
10. When you get toward the end of your life how will you have wished that you lived it?

*This is an interesting question to ask your Gen Y employees if you are of a different generation, because you will probably find that your Gen Y employees will identify people that they know who have impacted their own lives while Boomers and Veterans tend to identify icons and people who have made larger social changes.

Important note: If you are a supervisor or manager that has several new hires and has no time to meet with everyone individually, you can do this task with a large group of people by creating a "getting to know you" situation. More specifically, have all new hires and supervisors/managers line their chairs up across from each other and take time doing active listening using one or two of the questions, and then rotating to the next person. This activity is also a wonderful tool to use during a team-building retreat. During team-building retreats, depending on the size of the team, each person should have an opportunity to interview every person. The minimum amount of time allotted should be 20 minutes for each person; however, the more time the better.

Why it works

This is a wonderful activity that teaches your Gen Y employees how to actively listen to people, which is a skill that has not been developed well in this generation because the focus has been on listening to the self rather than listening to others. This is an invaluable skill that if practiced enough, will eventually become automatic and help develop your Gen Y employees' leadership skills. Honing your own active listening skills will also make you a more effective leader.

In addition, this technique helps develop some of the qualities of self-actualization that contribute to positive leadership skills and effective workplace functioning, such as:

> Enhanced self-awareness.
> Improved ability to think about different perspectives.
> Enhanced acceptance of others.
> Sensitivity to the needs of others.
> Development of meaningful relationships with others.
> Developing an understanding that each person has strengths and weaknesses and has the right to be heard.

Idea into action

During a recent team-building retreat, Dr. Lipkin used this activity to help develop the relationships among a generationally mixed, hardworking, stressed team. What was interesting during this task was that the team refused to keep within the time allotted for each interview. What was supposed to be a two-hour activity ended up taking three and a half hours, because everyone was enjoying their conversations and a group decision was made to allot more time. After a three month follow up, this task was cited as one of the most useful activities of the retreat. Many of the team members expressed that not only did they develop relationships but it also helped them start listening to one another more intently and more compassionately. Interestingly enough, two team members reported that they reduced the amount of e-mails they sent to their colleagues sitting in close-by offices and would get up to go talk to them in person instead when they could. Due to the improved relationships, it was also reported that productivity increased.

CS2: The ice cream sandwich

Are you wondering what ice cream sandwiches have to do with self-esteem and the corporate world? Ice cream sandwiches can be compared to communicating unpleasant feedback because the guilt of eating an ice cream sandwich can be outweighed by its fabulous taste and communicating necessary criticism can be outweighed by the comfort of real, positive feedback. If there is good, solid, real, and positive feedback when we are receiving constructive criticism we will be more likely to take it in (or eat it). Using this concept, consider redesigning your message when you give feedback to a Generation Y employee (or any other employee or anybody in your life). If you begin the message with a positive and affirmative statement, followed by the constructive criticism, followed by another positive and affirming statement, your message and feedback will be emotionally digested similar to an ice cream sandwich versus the emotional digestion of awful-tasting liquid cold medicine.

Remember though, it is important to give genuine positive feedback because inauthentic feedback, especially when positive, can cause more damage, especially among Generation Y employees. This savvy approach of the ice cream sandwich will hopefully lessen the impact of the blow to self-esteem that often accompanies criticism for Generation Y by cushioning the paralyzing effect of the criticism, and increasing adaptive self-esteem by providing genuine feedback based on real accomplishments.

Shrinkwrapped

The ice cream sandwich approach is based on Pendleton's rules for feedback (1984) that positive messages need to come before negative messages. It's based on the simple principle of the emotional bank balance (that is, withdrawals cannot be sustained without credits in place first). To try Pendleton's approach directly, use the following as a guide for giving feedback:

1. *Employee engages in self-assessment regarding their strengths or what they feel they do well.*

2. *Supervisor reinforces strengths identified, if they agree, and points out additional strengths if present.*

3. *The employee is asked to also identify areas for improvement.*

4. *Supervisor reinforces these areas for improvement and identifies additional developmental areas.*

(Pendleton, D., T. Shofield, P. Tate, P. Havelock. The Consultation: An approach to learning. Oxford: Oxford University Press, 1984)

Why it works

The ice cream sandwich approach to constructive criticism works because it's psychologically easier to hear criticism, or "negative" feedback, when you also get to hear that you are good and liked and that your work is appreciated. We offer constructive criticism and provide feedback to promote change, so if the constructive criticism is not heard, then changes will not be made. If feedback is not thoughtfully ingested with resulting plans for change then the building of adaptive self-esteem and motivation for change will not happen.

Important note: If you are concerned that the constructive criticism will be overshadowed by the positive feedback provided, brainstorm with your Gen Y an action plan of how to address the constructive criticism with clear action steps, expectations, and a timeline for follow through.

Idea into action

Dr. Lipkin and Dr. Perrymore challenged a small business owner whose Gen Y employees stated that they often felt that they were being judged to try the ice cream sandwich approach. This business owner was open to changing her approach, as she admitted that she has a habit of boldly stating what needed to be done differently without regard for how the message was received by her employee. This was never a problem for her until she began hiring more and more Gen Y employees. She was noticing that her Gen Y employees would start crying or become angry with her, and their behaviors would not change. She stated that she had a recurring problem with an employee who did not proofread her documents. She remembered that she had told this usually hardworking employee, "You can't hand stuff like this in," and her employee started crying. The problem continued, so when confronting this issue again she tried the ice cream sandwich approach and said the following: "I'm really impressed with your dedication to this project. You've clearly always put in a lot of time and effort, however. You need to proofread your documents before you pass them out in the committee meeting because it undermines the wonderful work you are doing." Her employee was better able to hear this feedback and her behavior changed.

Brainer coaching solutions

CS3: The 180: where real changes happen

The concept of a 360 assessment can be an invaluable tool when working with Gen Y to help them develop their abilities to digest feedback, especially constructive feedback, and gain insight into their strengths and developmental areas. It is one of the most common tools used in coaching. The reason why it is used so frequently is because it gives the coach and the coachee a well-rounded evaluation of the coachee's strengths and developmental areas from the perspective of different people with whom the coachee works (for example, their bosses, their subordinates, and their peers). Yeah, yeah, a 360 is nice, the name implies that it brings you back right to the same place and that's why we like to call it a 180.

How do you do it? We suggest identifying one or two managers who have contact with the employee and three peers, two from similar generations and one from another generation. Their feedback can be anonymous and perhaps the Gen Y employee undergoing the 180 process can make that decision. However, if they are given anonymity, explain that the purpose of the 180 is to give them accurate feedback to help them develop leadership skills, and they are likely to get more honest feedback if the feedback is anonymously given. Once this decision is made, create a questionnaire with open-ended questions that you distribute to the "180 team." You could also ask your gen Y if they have any questions that they would like to add, so that they can receive feedback on an aspect of their performance that they are concerned about. These questions should be related to a certain project that the individual worked on with a team of people. If the individual does not work on a team, then these questions should be related to a specific and definable period of time, so that your "180 team" has a specific range for feedback. Examples of open-ended questions could include:

1. After working with Y on the last project, what would you say was his/her most significant contribution?
2. What was the most difficult part about working with Y?
3. What was easy about working with Y?
4. What is the best quality about Y's communication style?
5. What is the most difficult quality about Y's communication style?
6. If you could change three aspects of Y's work performance, what would they be?
7. If you had to choose three aspects of Y's work performance that you feel make him/her shine, what would you say they are?
8. If you were Y's supervisor what would be the most difficult part to manage about him/her?
9. As Y's peer, what are the top three things you like about working with this person?

10. As Y's peer, what are the top three things that make it difficult about working with this person?

11. If you had to place Y on a forced ranking scale (every team member is placed on a scale from "exceeds performance" to "substandard performance" and every spot on the scale must be filled) where would you place Y and why? What can they do to improve their ranking (even if they are in the highest spot)?

After feedback is gathered, spend an hour reviewing the answers and organizing the 180 team's thoughts. Make sure that you understand the feedback before you present it. When you are presenting the feedback to your Gen Y employee make it clear that this is an exercise to help enhance their talents and that you are committed to working on the areas that they need to develop to help them progress in the company. When giving the constructive criticism, refer to the previous coaching solution, "The Ice Cream Sandwich," which will help you provide the feedback in the most constructive and digestible way possible. By giving this feedback in a planned meeting that the Gen Y expects (and is aware of its purpose) you are providing the Gen Y with an opportunity to take feedback, digest it, and develop his or her talents and weaknesses to become more productive and better at what they do.

Following the 180 feedback, develop a co-collaborative action plan with your Gen Y employee about the goals they are going to work on, based on the 180 feedback, and how you are going to support them to reach these goals. Define measurable action steps with clear timelines and steps. If possible, meet on a bi-monthly or monthly basis to assess these defined goals and tweak the action steps to make them doable, reachable, and sensible.

Important note: If your Gen Y employee has a poor reaction to the feedback you give, take a step back and ask them to provide you feedback about their reaction using active listening skills. Keep in mind that accepting feedback is difficult, especially in the workplace, and this is why using an outside consultant or coach may be your best bet when implementing the 180. Note that an outside consultant will usually refer to this process as a 360 assessment.

Why it works

A 180-degree interview is designed to help you develop your Gen Y employee based on real feedback that provides them with an opportunity to learn how others perceive them with regard to their strengths and developmental areas. Because the feedback is given in a supportive, positive manner, your Gen Y employee should tolerate the feedback better and work with you to define targets and goals that can be accomplished. The important part of this is that it will help them start seeing themselves in a realistic light, help them manage their unrealistic expectations, help them become more independent and autonomous, and begin developing insight into their own capabilities. These are all qualities that can help them pave the way toward self-actualization.

CS4: Self-expression versus self-control: insert thought here.

Gen Y was raised to speak their minds no matter what, no matter when, no matter how. Obviously, this is not always the best thing in the workplace, especially when all you want is for them to be more verbally reserved. Observably, this generation is strong in "self-expression." However, they often lack "self-control," which creates problems in the workplace. Issues of self-control often come from an inability to insert thought before action. So, helping Gen Y learn this skill (herein termed "insert thought here") can be incredibly helpful and help them internalize self-control, which will ultimately impact their effectiveness and productivity. Pulling from cognitive behavioral techniques, often used in therapeutic settings, we suggest asking your Gen Y employee the following questions after you feel they have acted without the "insert thought here" mechanism:

1. When you did/said ABC, what were you feeling at the time?
2. When you did/said ABC, what were you thinking? (This is not to be asked in a derogatory manner, but rather in a questioning, "Let's discover your thoughts together" manner.)
3. When you did/said ABC, what was the outcome you wanted to achieve?
4. What alternative steps could you have taken to achieve the outcome you wanted?
5. What steps can you take now to move toward the positive outcome you hoped for?

Important note: To avoid hearing several "I don't know," answers, it will be important to explain to your Gen Y employee that this is a brainstorming exercise. Advise them to just say whatever comes to mind when the question is asked, even if they feel the answer doesn't make much sense. Let them know that you will work together as a team to flesh out viable solutions.

Why it works

"Insert thought here" takes a negative situation and turns it into an action-oriented solution with steps to move toward accomplishing a goal. It provides a framework to help your Gen Y begin developing (or improving) self-control.

Big-brainer coaching solutions

CS5: Shifting from self-centered to issue centered using SWOT

With the self-inflation movement, Gen Ys often make organizational decisions via a self-focused lens, which can impact the health of an organization or team. Helping them become more issue centered rather than self-centered is an important process in grooming your Gen Y employees. When you help people shift from a self-perspective to an issue centered perspective, or what we like to call a holistic perspective, you have more of a chance of shifting their focus and decision-making processes from a self-focused perspective to a greater good perspective. It is also important to help them see and become concerned about problems that do not directly affect them, but rather affect the organization. Why is this important? When people are willing to think about how their actions impact their coworkers, their bosses, their organizations, and the relationship of the organization to the environment, they are more apt to make decisions informed by an idea of holism (all parts are connected) versus decisions based on self-focused ideals, perspectives, and platforms.

You can help your Gen Y employees begin integrating the concept of holism into their general, day-to-day decision-making processes, by encouraging them to think through problems using a classic decision-making process: (SWOT). SWOT is an acronym for Strengths, Weakness, Opportunity, and Threats developed by Albert Humphrey, a business and management consultant. A desired goal or objective needs to be decided on, and once the desired goal or objective is formed, SWOT requires:

1) Brainstorm the potential **S**trengths and **W**eaknesses associated with the problem and decision as it pertains to the:
   a. Organization.
   b. Team.
   c. Individual.

2) Brainstorm the **O**pportunities and **T**hreats of a problem and a decision as it pertains to the:
   a. Organization.
   b. Team.
   c. Individual.

This can be applied to general goal and target setting too. More specifically, as a supervisor, you can help your Gen Y employees develop motivation to clearly define their own measures of excellence and quality performance with respect to the larger organizational goals. With these ideas outlined, you can coach and guide them to weigh their opportunities and threats and plan risk taking with regard to their decisions, judgments, and actions all while incorporating a holistic approach.

Why it works

Although this sounds time consuming, going through this process one time with a person may be enough to teach them the importance of shifting from a self-focused, need-based perspective to a perspective that incorporates decision-making for the greater good. Along the way, what you start developing or grooming in your Gen Y employee is an even stronger sense of social consciousness, stronger organizational commitment, and the enhancement (or development) of an achievement orientation—a quality that is inherently aligned with excellent leadership.

CS6: Turning the self-inflation movement into a self-actualization movement

Abraham Maslow, a humanistic psychologist, theorized that basic needs must be met before we can strive toward self-actualization or achieving our full potential, a concept relevant to the development and maintenance of our successful business and personal identities. Being on the path of striving toward maximizing one's own potential is an important part of growing up and a crucial component of becoming a great leader. Of course, Maslow theorized that only 1 percent of the population ever achieves self-actualization. However, the important lessons learned in life are taught during the journey rather than the arrival at the destination.

Although achieving self-actualization is a lifelong process, we believe that identifying your Gen Y top talent now and investing in their future to help them move toward self-actualization will shape their leadership potential and ultimately, the future of your organization. Once you have identified your top Gen Y talent, we recommend investing in a leadership coach to hone their strengths, address their personal developmental areas, and concentrate on the enhancement of self-actualizing qualities. The following are characteristics reflective of self-actualized individuals within the workplace that are not simply positive characteristics to strive for personally, but qualities representative of excellent leadership and effective work relationships:

> Realistic and practical approach to their work.
> Acceptance of self and others, free of judgment.
> Independent with regard to thinking, emotions, and behavior, and willing to be accountable.
> Issue-centered rather than self-centered.
> Needs and appreciates time for solitude and reflection.
> Independent and autonomous.
> Has experienced peak personal and professional experience.
> Sensitive to the needs of others around them, feeling of togetherness.
> Non-hostile sense of humor.
> Have and values deep, meaningful experiences with people.
> Understands that each person has strengths and weaknesses, and believes that everyone has the right to be heard.
> Enjoys the process not just the end result or the goal.
> High level of creativity.
> Values individuality.
> Understands that they are imperfect and strives toward continued growth.

Why it works

When you identify the talent you want to groom for future leadership roles early on, you can begin to help them develop the skills necessary for successful personal and professional identities. Leadership coaches are often hired to assist those in top-level management positions. However, investing in your young, talented Gen Y's is not only a wise decision for the future of the company, it is an investment that will help engage and retain the employees that you want to keep.

Coaching solutions simplified

Coaching Solution 1

Title: Turning the "I am, I did, I want" into "tell me more about you" conversation.

Purpose: To get to know your Generation Y (and other) staff and enhancing their listening skills.

Outcome: Relationship building, team building, development of listening skills, enhancement of leadership skills.

Coaching Solution 2

Title: The ice cream sandwich.

Purpose: To provide genuine feedback and increase ability to accept constructive criticism to develop skills.

Outcome: Constructive criticism that is heard and implemented, relationship building, and increased realistic self-reflection.

Coaching Solution 3

Title: The 180: where real changes happen.

Purpose: To help your Gen Y employees gain insight into how their behaviors and actions impact the team and impact their own progress and successes at work.

Outcome: Enhanced ability to accept constructive feedback, strength building, improved self-awareness, and action planning for developmental areas.

Coaching Solution 4

Title: Self-expression versus self-control: insert thought here.

Purpose: To help Gen Y employees think through situations in more critical and analytical ways, so that their decisions are organizationally beneficial rather than self-focused and/or impulsive.

Outcome: Enhanced self-control, better decision-making abilities, improved organizational judgment, and relationship building.

Coaching Solution 5

Title: Shifting from self-centered to issue-centered using SWOT.

Purpose: To help your Gen Y employees shift from a self-centered and self-focused mindset to a more holistic and organizationally inclusive mindset.

Outcome: Enhanced emotional awareness, improved relationships, increased organizational efficacy with improved decision-making.

Coaching Solution 6

Title: Turning the self-inflation movement into a self-actualization movement.

Purpose: To identify top Gen Y talent and invest in their professional growth by hiring a leadership coach to help them move toward self-actualization in the workplace, hone their strengths and work on developmental areas.

Outcome: Leadership development.

——Chapter 3——

Helicopters, Hoverers, Boomerangs, and Parachutes? Generation Y and Their Parents

Parents often talk about the younger generation as if they didn't have anything to do with it.

—Haim Ginott (1922–1973), Psychologist

> *"As a former recruiter with extensive experience hiring interns and entry-levels, I have seen helicopter parents drop off resumes at career fairs, visit HR to schedule an interview for their kid, call me to find out their kids' status in the search, and even argue for their kid when they don't get a job. I personally always pushed back at parents and insist on only dealing with the kid. Now I am a career coach specializing in Gen Y, so these helicopter parents are sometimes my economic buyers. Many parents are working their hardest at getting the right balance of supporting and encouraging their child and not being overbearing during this very difficult market. But my service exists because parents are heavily investing in their kids and trying to give them every advantage in life, including the job search."*
> *Caroline Ceniza-Levine, co-founder,*
> *SixFigureStart*

A unique phenomenon that began with the emergence of Generation Y is the idea of "helicopter" parents, hovering and acting on behalf of their children with good intentions of protection, but resulting in stunting their children's independent growth and ability to make mistakes and learn from them. This type of behavior in the corporate environment has left leaders amazed, bewildered, and concerned for the future with questions of how a Generation Y employee could possibly become a CEO of a company if the mothers and fathers are still metaphorically packing their lunches and dressing them in the morning.

Of course not every parent or caregiver behaves this way, but high parental and community protection has created a sense of dependence and false sense of security that mom and dad can fix everything and anything. This results in an inability to cope with failure or roadblocks. So, when a Generation Y employee is upset, whether it is because of an interview for a job or a bad day at the office, expect mom and dad to know about it. Although Gen Y's have a strong sense of self-value with an indirect motto of, "I make my own decisions, I am the boss of me (what do you think Mom and Dad?)," it is important that this generation learn how to become more autonomous, instead of having life stressors and roadblocks removed by their parents without the opportunity to independently develop effective coping skills. The presence of helicopter parents in the workplace has created several difficulties in the work lives of Generation Y and the companies they work for. Due to a generation-wide problem-solving approach where the way to solve a problem is to ask mom or dad to fix it, there has been a major decrease in independence, reduced accountability, and a lack of responsibility taking in their personal and professional lives. Furthermore, it has often harmed their reputations in professional settings, as it is difficult to take an employee seriously when their mother or father just contacted you on their son or daughter's behalf.

The benefit of helicopter parenting is that parents and children share a close relationship with a continuance of support and encouragement throughout the lifespan to keep Generation Y motivated and positive. Despite this positive quality, Generation Y would benefit from the development of a parachute so that they can begin making their own way and develop a healthy sense of independence, which will ultimately enhance their leadership potential.

Back to the (psychological) basics

Helicopter parents: how did it happen?

No other generation in history was as wanted and as cherished as Generation Y. The culture and environment in which this generation was raised was the most child-centric among all other generations. Their parents have had a strong powerful presence in the lives (and work) decisions of their Gen Y children/

adults. In many respects, Generation Y is coping well with their prolonged child-hoods. They are closer to their parents than any other generation, and they have what seems like unwavering respect and value for their parent's opinions. They treasure their friendships with their parents and their parents are often the first people they contact when faced with a difficult challenge. Helicopter parents have fostered this type of relationship with their children because they have difficulty letting go and forcing their Gen Y adult children to make it in the world alone. After all, they have spent enormous amounts of devotion, time, money, and effort raising their perfect "can-do-no-wrong" adult children.

Shrinkwrapped

The term "helicopter parents" was coined by Foster W. Cline, MD and Jim Fay in their book titled Parenting with Love and Logic *(first published in 1990, most recently published in 2006). They discussed the difference between what they called "helicopter parents" (who hover above their children) and "drill sergeant parents" (who order their children around). Cline and Fay state that neither parenting style contributes to positive growth and both styles fail when it comes to providing useful parenting advice.*

Although the term "helicopter parenting" was originated in the 1990s, by the year 2000, as Generation Y's numbers increased on college campuses, college professors and college administrations became quite aware of the term "helicopter parenting" and the widespread phenomenon of parental intrusion in the lives of their "adult" children. These are the parents who called their college-aged children to wake them up in the morning to make it to work or class on time. They have also been known to argue with teachers about the grades their children have received or to call their adult child's boss to tell them they are disappointed in the results of their son's or daughter's performance review. These hovering parents, coming from a place of good intentions, have lost perspective that their job was to guide their children to become independent thinkers and learn from their mistakes.

Did this really happen? Yes!

E. Wade, a professor at a four-year college, assigned a research paper to be completed throughout the course of the college semester. He stated that one of his students handed in the paper using references from Vogue and also references from some popular movies, including Legally Blonde *(a 2001*

> *movie where a blond sorority girl goes to law school to win back her boy-friend who recently ended their relationship). Not only were inadequate references used, the paper was written poorly and the student earned a low grade to reflect her poor performance. Shortly after handing back the pa-pers, he received a phone call from the student's mother questioning the grading criteria used and demanding to see some kind of documentation reflecting what was expected of the student. He told us that trying to explain that the paper was poorly written and that movies and popular fashion magazines are not appropriate references for a college research paper was a futile argument, so he faxed over the description of the requirements for the research paper as the mother requested.*

Many parents have a difficult time seeing the negative consequences that helicopter parenting can have on their children. It is the way they have always been with their children, so it is difficult to stop behaving this way even though their child may be 25 years old. A perfect example of the type of negative consequences from helicopter parents' over-protective and over-bearing behav-ior is the reaction the professor in the previous story had toward the student after the interaction with her mother. The professor told us that it was almost impossible to treat the student like an adult after the incident, and he found that he was using kid gloves when communicating with the student. In addi-tion, the professor shared with us that it was really hard to find respect for the student following that interaction. This was particularly difficult for the pro-fessor, because his approach was to treat his adult college students like adults who are responsible for their own work and their own behaviors.

No one wants to see those whom they love struggling or in any type of pain. However, to deny the opportunity to fully confront and manage disap-pointments, mishaps, and struggles is to deny the opportunity to develop adaptive coping skills and personal strengths. Not having the opportunity to learn and experience for one's self has set Generation Y up for letdowns and disappointments that have the potential to be devastating. As much as parents may try to protect their Gen Y children from hardships, the truth of the mat-ter is that it is simply impossible. Consequently, what is left is a generation ill equipped to deal with the realities of life and ultimately a generation with doubts about their abilities, struggling with their identities and purpose in life.

> **Shrinkwrapped**
>
> *When problems are solved by others rather than having to personally struggle through them and learn from them, not only do we lack the necessary learning of how to cope with conflicts, stress, and dilemmas, throughout time we lack the development of accountability for our problems and choices. We may continue to state responsibility for something that has occurred, but it is never taken the step further where we understand our part in the dilemma or conflict and grow from it.*

Effects of helicopter parenting in the workplace

> *"I once had a job candidate show up to the interview with her mother. I interviewed the candidate as quickly as possible (not in the presence of the mother) and sent her on her way, as there was no chance at all I was interested in hiring someone who had her MOTHER show up with her at a job interview."*
> *Maria, director of communications,*
> *Higher Education Industry*

A long-term side effect of helicopter parenting is that the protection that these adults received as children (and continue to receive as adults) resulted in a lack of experiencing intense pain, understanding of personal fault, and poor ability to handle and learn from mistakes. This has had a disastrous impact in the workplace. The following is a list of problems stemming from the consequence of helicopter parenting and actual statements from bosses attesting to these workplace problems:

Inability to independently make decisions and problem-solve: "My dad thinks we should charge this much and my dad thinks we should go after such and such client next. "What about what the Gen Yer thinks?"

Claudia Ross, owner,

Cross Marketing

Lack of confidence in dealing with workplace problems and life stressors, which is acquired by conquering difficult situations and developing coping skills. Instead everything becomes a crisis: "I can't come to work for the next few days because my boyfriend broke up with me."

Kristen Lutz, advertising executive,

Advertising Industry

Lack of autonomy: "I showed the contract of employment to my father and he suggested that you change this or he says I shouldn't work here."

Claudia Ross, owner,

Cross Marketing

Lack of accountability: "It's not my fault!" Even though they were the only employee in charge of that task.

Charles G., sales director,

Telecommunications Industry

Lack of responsibility and follow through: Instead of the Gen Y employee calling, her mother calls her boss and says, "My daughter won't be able to come to work today because of a family engagement where her presence is mandatory."

Douglas M., HR director,

Utility Industry

Although there are clearly negative results in the workplace due to helicopter parenting, this generation has the advantage of sharing a close relationship/friendship with their parents, and this has resulted in setting the foundation for close relationships with their bosses (who are often the same age as their parents). Due to this close relationship, they are comfortable with and feel warmth toward their parents' generation. To understand how this naturally occurs, it's important to understand the concept of transference.

Shrinkwrapped

Transference was coined by Sigmund Freud to describe a relationship dynamic that occurs between patients and psychoanalysts during a session, where a patient's thoughts and feelings about their parents are subconsciously endowed or transferred onto their analyst/therapist. Today, transference is frequently talked about outside of the therapy room, and is witnessed when one places their thoughts, feelings, or expectations of a significant person in their life onto someone else. This is thought to occur without our conscious awareness.

If this sounds like psychobabble to you just think about your own life. If you have a great relationship with your sister, then you might feel warmly toward someone you meet who reminds you of your sister. This happens all the time and within the context of all the various types of relationships we have with those in our lives. For Generation Y it is not as simple, because they want their bosses to be their parents and mentor them; this is the result of transference. If you have children yourself, think about the employees that are close to the ages of your children. Do you ever notice that you see them in a different light? You are apt to subconsciously offer a little more warmth toward them if they remind you of your child. Now here's some psychobabble for you: The reaction that you are experiencing in response to your employees based on the transference they have placed onto you is called countertransference.

A leader says:

Kevin Mercuri, president of Propheta Communications relayed to us, "Sometimes my wife tells me I am Gen Y's surrogate father because I end up hearing most of their personal lives and end up giving advice. They are used to having a parent figure around."

This transference-countertransference phenomenon that goes on in the workplace highlights another long-term consequence of helicopter parenting. Because Gen Y's parents have always taken care of their needs and have always had their adult children's backs, even if they were in the wrong, Gen Y has pretty high expectations. This can be a problem, especially when most bosses are not interested in babysitting their Gen Y employees or giving them concessions, but are interested in developing their skills and increasing their independence.

Did this really happen? Yes!

Stevie Ray, executive director of Stevie Ray's Improv Company, told us that one of his Gen Y employees asked him for a raise because he had really high car payments. Stevie told his Gen Y employee that he needed to do more work in order to earn extra money, and his Gen Y employee exclaimed, "But what about my car payments?"

Y in the Workplace

Another problem stemming from transference in the workplace is the lack of formality that occurs when a Gen Y is communicating with upper management. This happens because the parents of Gen Y revolted against the traditional family hierarchy that they were raised under, and, instead, raised their Gen Y children to have open lines of communication and form friend relationships with their parents. Generation Y has naturally transferred this comfort level with their parents to their relationships with their supervisors and other coworkers. This informality can be shocking for other generations as they hear their Gen Y coworkers and supervisee's say things that most outside of Generation Y would consider inappropriate. (For example, "ugh, I drank way too much last night," "I had to call out, I just got my period and have cramps," "I just had the best sex this morning," and so on). Generation Y's informality and candor is often seen as a lack of respect and lack of workplace etiquette. However, it can also be seen as comfort and openness with others, regardless of age and status. This has resulted in a change in the workplace with Generation Y rapidly challenging and changing long standing corporate social formality.

Along with the change in candor that Generation Y has brought to the workplace, they have also been challenging employee-supervisor relationships in interesting ways. Generation Y is comfortable with all age groups and their bosses are no more intimidating to them than their parents' best friend whom they have always talked to informally. This can be challenging for Gen Y supervisors who often wonder where the respect went. Generation Y does not believe that the boss is the boss, and is to be respected. They believe that the boss is the boss and is there to help them, offer assistance, and earn respect just like everybody else. They do not want to be seen as just an employee, they want to be valued. They are not interested in just having a boss; they want a mentor. Demanding? Yes! But there is a trade off for their supervisors. Once a Generation Y employee bonds with their supervisor, they are extremely loyal. This loyalty to their supervisors surpasses their loyalty to a company.

A Gen Y says:

"Early on in my career, I worked for this incredible company that I really liked and had the best boss ever. Unfortunately he left for a different job. I initially stayed on with the company because I liked it so much, but after that boss left, the job was never the same. I ended up following him to his new company and that's where I am today."

J.D. Haldin, art director,

Software Development and Web Design Company

Boomerang Y's

Families are closer today than ever before. College graduates often want to or have to move back in with their families after college, and their parents are accepting them with open arms. This is so common that it even has a term: boomeranging (note that this term is also used to describe people who leave the workforce and come back). A boomerang launches and then comes back. The same seems to be true of Generation Y. They launch their way to college, travel a bit, and then come back home to shack up with their parents. This is quite a change from the boomer generation (the Y's parents) who were married in their late teens/early 20s and moved out of their parents' house as soon as they could to create their own families.

Boomeranging has become so prevalent due to a problematic economy, difficulty finding suitable jobs, enormous school debt, and skyrocketing housing prices. For some Gen Y's, living with their parents is a necessity for financial reasons, and for others it is a preference to be with their parents on a daily basis. There is another group of Gen Y's who continue to live with their parents into their adult years because they are not making their expected high salary right out of college and cannot imagine lowering the standard of living to which they are accustomed. What has resulted is a prolonged adolescence stage among this generation, because they have had the greatest opportunity of all generations to attend college coupled with the ability to boomerang back home after college. More specifically, they can be kids for a longer period of time and take longer to decide what they "really" want to do with their lives. Ask a Gen Y when they felt like they were finally a "grown up," taking care of themselves independently (financially, emotionally, vocationally, socially), and you'll no doubt be surprised by their answers—"Still doing it!"

Boomeranging in the workplace

Due to the boomerang effect many Gen Y's have more than a solid parental support system; they have a live-in problem-solving system. This can be wonderful, unless their problem-solving consultant is telling them that whatever happened, whatever the conflict, it's not their fault, and that it will be taken care of. Throughout their lives, many of those in Generation Y have been shielded from taking accountability and responsibility for their actions. When you lack the ability to step back and take responsibility for the behaviors that you chose to engage in, you lack the ability to gain insight into how you impact others and your environment, and you also lose out on learning from your choices, mistakes, and accomplishments. Responsibility and accountability-taking is one of the most important skills that one develops in childhood and continues to refine as an adult. Not only does it help you monitor your actions, it contributes to the ongoing development of one's personal and professional goals and purpose. When people choose not to be responsible and accountable for their life course, behaviors, and actions, they tend to struggle in their level of commitment to their actions and their overall direction. Not only has this quality impacted the quality of their work functioning, it has also negatively impacted the perception of their generation among their other generation coworkers.

Additionally, if we have all of our basic needs (that is, food, shelter, and so on) met as an adult by someone else who has always taken care of us, asking nothing in return, then we lack lessons learned that come hand-in-hand with life responsibilities, and are more likely to say, "Take this job and shove it!" It's easy to take dissatisfaction with work, with a boss, or with a coworker, and jump ship with thoughts of "I do not need this frustration" and "I have no reason that I need to work here." What is lost is the lesson learned from working through difficult situations and sticking with a problem to its resolution. This impacts one's ability to follow through with responsibility and ultimately impacts one's ability to handle responsibility in the workplace.

Three advantages of Generation Y's relationship with their parents

"Whenever I held my newborn baby in my arms, I used to think that what I said and did to him could have an influence not only on him, but on all whom he met, not only for a day or a month or a year, but for all eternity—a very challenging and exciting thought for a mother."

—Rose Kennedy (1890–1995)

I always have someone on my side (no matter what)

With their close family, Generation Y has the benefit of continued familial support and encouragement. Right or wrong, appropriate or inappropriate, their parents are on their side. If they have a bad day, a conflict with a co-worker, or dissatisfaction with an assignment their boss has given them, their parents are there to comfort and console them in a safe place of parental warmth. Helicopter parents are caring people and offer love and support to their children. Having this type of support and love can make one feel as though they can conquer anything. It's a good feeling to know that no matter what, someone in the world has your back. In the best case scenario, Generation Ys and their helicopter parents are a powerful force. However, leaders in the workplace will need to motivate their Gen Y employees to develop parachutes so they can become more independent, solve their own conflicts, and confront their own problems.

HR chimes in:

"During interviews I usually ask the candidate to tell me about their heroes. More than any other generation, Gen Y's will state that one of their parents serves as one of their heroes."
Felicia Smith, VP of human resources,
Large Medical Equipment Company

Parental guidance offers wisdom that same-aged peers cannot give

When a problem, stress, or a crisis presents at work, your Generation Y employee will be on the phone with their parents asking for their guidance. Sure they talk to their friends when they need guidance and support. However, their parents are a major part of their support system. At its best, the guidance given from parents of Gen Y allows for supportive feedback based on wisdom gained from their parents' experiences at work. In addition, when a parent is serving as a support, rather than an interfering helicopter parent, they often provide good perspective on various workplace issues.

A Gen Y says:

Keri, a Gen Y employee, told us, "I respect my mom's opinion more than anyone else and call her when I need advice. She knows everything and she's almost always right too."

Boss, I like you—you remind me of my mom/dad

The majority of Generation Y has extremely positive relationships with their parents, and the majority of Generation Y's supervisors are the same age as their parents. Remember the concept of transference? What may occur is a positive relationship between Gen Y and their boss based on the fact that their boss resembles their parent and they understand and relate well to their parents' generation. When this happens, relationships at work can develop quickly across generations. Although this is an advantage, it is important to note that problems can develop if the Gen Y employee has the expectation that they will be treated the same by their boss as they are by their parents. That being said, for Gen Y positive feelings and good relationships with their boss have the tendency to develop quickly.

A leader says:

"As their supervisor I end up playing parent and helping them avoid the small hurdlers. For example, I shield them from angry clients, because if they get yelled at they will shut down for two days and get really upset."
Kevin Mercuri, president,
Propheta Communications

How it plays out in the workplace: three challenges of Generation Y's relationship with their parents

"The problem with children is that you have to put up with their parents."
—Charles DeLint, writer (1951–)

Mom and Dad don't always have the answer? Neither does my boss?

Yes, it would be great if we could take all of our problems to the metaphorical wise old man on top of the mountain and leave with great solutions to all of our dilemmas. However, we all know that too many problems exist, solutions are required quickly, and that metaphorical old man has been replaced with Google and Ask.com. For the most part though, Generation Y has had parents who have personally fixed their dilemmas. This is difficult for parents to stop doing once their child begins college and continues to be difficult for some Gen Y parents as their adult child begins their career. This has resulted in some Gen Y parents calling their adult child's place of employment with the purpose of resolving their dilemma. Gen Y employees also often look to their supervisors to fix a problem that they are having, and be unconditionally supportive and on their side while helping them. This has resulted in many supervisors being asked by their Gen Y employees to help them resolve personal problems, bail them out of their mistakes, or intervene in workplace conflict.

A leader says:

J. Joyce, a Marketing Director of a large retail chain told us that one of her Gen Y employees came to her to complain about a "conflict" she was having with one of her more senior coworkers who was serving as the team lead. When Mrs. Joyce asked what the conflict was her Gen Y employee said, "she's telling me what to do and bossing me around." Mrs. Joyce suggested to her Gen Y employee that she talk to her coworker about this and resolve the conflict and reminded her Gen Y employee that her coworker was actually the team lead and responsible for "bossing her around." Her Gen Y employee refused to deal with the "conflict" without Mrs. Joyce getting involved.

Hold please, I need to take this call…it's my mom

The days of parents dropping off their children at college and then not seeing them again until the first holiday break are ongoing. Frequent communication with parents continues in the workplace, with constant contact throughout some workdays and sometimes even during important meetings. There is an openness among this generation about the important role their parents play in their lives and an expectation that this will be tolerated and allowed, even if it is treated as more important than other workplace responsibilities. In fact, Gen Y's are inviting their parents to show up at work to meet their bosses. Although this is sometimes tolerated and welcomed, it is often jarring, unexpected, and confusing for upper management.

A Gen Y says:

Christina, a Gen Y legal assistant for a law firm, stated the following: "I had my mom stop by work to meet my boss a few weeks ago. It's important for her to see what my work is like so she can give me advice when I need it."

I don't need money—I have someone who can cover my bills

Although Generation Y individuals have bills (at the very least credit cards resulting from offers the minute they step onto college campuses), their happiness at work is more important then the bills they may have to pay. When your parents are willing to bail you out no matter what, it is easier to stray away from your responsibilities and quit your job to find the next "dream" job. Sure it is great that parents are there to help; however, this is a generation that would benefit from some staying power, roughing it through the hard times, and learning how to manage their own conflicts and disappointments by developing their coping skills and enhancing their ability to delay their own gratification.

HR chimes in:

"Generation Y does not share the value of lifelong loyalty to a company. This generation seems like they will leave a job once they feel they have received all they can from a particular position."
Douglas M., HR director,
Utility Company

The takeaways so far....

If you remember nothing else, take away the following:

> Generation Y values their relationships/friendships with their parents more so than every generation that preceded them.

> Helicopter parents have been known to inappropriately advocate on behalf of their Gen Y adult children in the workplace.

> Due to financial difficulties and/or personal preferences, many Gen Y college graduates move back in with their parents after college, which ultimately impacts responsibility and accountability taking.

You can use Gen Y's strong bond with their parents to your advantage by:

> Utilizing their "I can conquer anything" attitudes based on the incredible family support they have always received.

> Understanding that their parents can offer them solid advice based on their wisdom and experience.

> Being aware of the transference and countertransference that can occur between you and your Gen Y employees.

Due to Gen Y's strong relationship with their parents watch out for their tendency to:

> Look to you and other supervisors, who are more seasoned in the field, to solve their professional and personal problems.

> Have a strong parental presence at your office via consistent communication during the work day or in some cases visits to the office.

> Leave a job instead of resolve a conflict that arises if they have family financial and emotional security Gen Y's.

Now it's time to take some action. Here are the coaching solutions that we recommend to enhance the positives and manage the negatives regarding Gen Y's relationship with their helicopter parents.

Coaching solutions: building on strengths and addressing the challenge

The impact of helicopter parents and the boomerang effect are in full force in our workplaces. Are you ready to learn how to cope with the fact that by hiring a Gen Y employee you may have also hired their parents? Use the following coaching solutions to get to know your Gen Y's important family members, build strong supervisory relationships, set appropriate boundaries and clear expectations for Gen Y and their parents, and assist your Gen Y employees to develop their parachutes by helping them to build autonomy and increase their personal responsibility.

No-brainer coaching solutions

CS1: Friend and family day

Because family is important to almost everyone, incorporate opportunities for employees to bring their families and friends to organizational events.

Alternatively, create special opportunities and events that allow your employees to learn more about one another by including the people that are most important to them. Allowing this not only satisfies your Gen Y's desire for others to know them beyond their work, but it satisfies everyone's desire to be known for more than just their job title. Business should not always be just business, it is also personal, because people's lives outside of work matter, and this concept supports the positive Gen Y preference for fluidity between work and life.

Why it works

People inherently want to be understood and recognized for all the aspects that make them unique and special. Work is important, but it is only one part of our identity. Having the opportunity to include the people that matter to you the most and integrate them with people who you spend so much time with at work will enhance one's experience of work being integrated with life, which is a win-win solution. In addition, the more you know about someone outside of work, the more you are able to understand why they are the way they are and why they do the things they do. Understanding people at this deeper level ultimately enhances relationship building and trust, two components that are imperative in the workplace. Further, taking interest in your employees outside of work demonstrates investment in their interests and really shows a level of care and respect for their lives, which goes a long way in enhancing the supervisor-employee bond, as well as the bond between colleagues.

Idea into action

Kathy, founder/president of a family owned wine business, with mostly Gen Y's employees, said that although her company does not have any formal events for family and friends of employees, she makes it a point to show interest in her supervisees' families and offers to meet her Gen Y employees' family members should they wish to stop by. Although her cohorts with similar businesses tease her about her encouragement and willingness to schedule meetings with her Gen Y employees' family members, she reminds them that it does not take a lot of time, visits with family members are pleasant for the most part, and there is the added benefit of another layer of support if their parents visit the office and like what they see. In addition, she feels that this enhances the trust and respect between her and her employees, because this small effort demonstrates that she cares about them.

CS2: Be there and go there

As a boss to Generation Y, chances are you are probably older than them. You may even have children close to the age of your Gen Y employees. Due to the age difference, there is a tendency to see your Generation Y employees as green with a lot to learn. Although this may be true, remember that your Gen Y employees have spent their entire lives being an important person in the room with adults. So although they demand respect in a way it has never been demanded before, most Generation Y's value their supervisor's opinion and want to and expect to have a positive relationship with them. Supervisors, it is up to you to facilitate this relationship. It is easy. All you have to do is "be there" and "go there." "Be there" by listening to your Gen Y employees and being fully present with them during your conversations together. "Go there" by taking that extra step and spending time together outside of the office on at least a quarterly basis. In addition, organize a yearly activity to spend time outside of the office with a small group of supervisees, whether that is for a team building retreat or a team dinner. Talk to your Gen Y employees about your world outside of work. Let them get to know you as a human being with a life. However, we do recommend limiting your connection with your Gen Y employees on social networking sites such as Facebook and Twitter, as we all know communication via digital media sources can breed miscommunication and misunderstood intentions. Although this may appear to be a simple solution, most supervisors do not take the time to do it even though this approach to management goes a long way not only with building your relationship with your supervisees, but with enhancing loyalty and commitment to the organization.

Important note: Stay within your own comfort zone when revealing information about yourself. We are not suggesting that you have to be an open book. Conversely, it is important for you as a manager/supervisor to be cognizant of people's boundaries. Although we recommend getting to know your Gen Y's (and other employees) outside of their work identities, pay attention to limits people are setting with you and respect those limits and comfort zones.

A leader says:

"Remember if you want respect and accountability you have to lead with respect and accountability. The first step is getting to know whom you are working with and letting them get to know you."
Charles G., sales director,
Telecommunications industry

Why it works

The most effective way for Gen Y to feel valued at work is to receive positive feedback and to develop interpersonal closeness with their supervisors and colleagues. Taking time out of your day to develop your relationships with your employees is not exclusive of business/work; it is an integral part of good business management. Remember, Gen Y shows loyalty to people, not companies. The better the relationship with the boss, the more loyal the Gen Y employee.

Idea into action

Kent Lewis, president of Anvil Media relayed the importance of spending time with Generation Y stating, "They cannot be seen as second class citizens, if you are not connecting with them on a personal level there will be problems." He stated that while he has responsibilities at home, spending time with his Gen Y employees over coffee, dinner, and informal meetings, has created a sense of trust and respect between him and his Gen Y employees with the added benefits of increased work productivity, better relationships, and a new ease in communicating difficult feedback to them.

Brainer coaching solutions

CS3: When it comes to the families, beat 'em or join 'em

Managers, what do you do with those parents who call your office and demand to talk with you about your Gen Y supervisee? Yes, the decision is actually yours and/or your company's. You can beat them or join them when it comes to the amount of presence families/parents have in the workplace.

To beat them put privacy policies in place. We know that you are shocked by having to include a policy stating that bosses will not communicate with family members about employee status, progress, or conflict. However, new policies are always put in place when they become necessary, and starting yesterday, it became necessary. We suggest that you beat 'em (or put policies in place) while you also join 'em by adding recognition to the importance that families of origin have within the workplace to your Gen Y employees.

Joining them can be done with minimal effort by adding information for parents/families in a new hire packet. If you create a new hire packet with a family section, we suggest that the information you add includes expectations regarding parental contact with regard to your new hire, along with information outlining the importance of their assistance with increasing their child's independence and success in their careers. With regard to organizational policies, make it clear that it is not appropriate to take personal non-emergency calls at work if that is a policy you feel is necessary to enforce. Also, make it clear in your policies that issues related to employee performance will only be discussed with relevant parties within the workplace. Overall, if you help your Gen Y employees transform their relationships with their parents in their physical space at work, they will be able to float with their parachutes with less reliance on their parents' hovering while they are at work.

Why it works

Providing information to educate families of your Gen Y hires helps everyone know and understand the ground rules. Through enforced policies expectations can be set and followed.

Big-brainer coaching solutions

CS4: *Helping Gen Y's pack their parachutes and make their own lunches*

Remember: Parents are over-involved in your Gen Y employee's work life because they love them and want them to be successful. However, your job as a manager is not to coach parents on how to help their children become more independent and successful in their careers and their life (as much as you may want to). Your job as a supervisor and manager is to inspire your Generation Y employee to want more independence and personal power to enhance their careers and increase their chances of success. How do you do this after 25 years of lunches being packed, backseat driving running rampant, and umbilical cords tied tightly around every decision-making process? Here are our suggestions:

› When you present your Gen Y employee with a problem, spend time brain storming solutions with them. Allow them time with you or near you to come up with the best solution and provide a reason why. Initially sit with them so that they develop some confidence in their abilities to create useful, productive, and effective solutions, thereby incrementally providing them with confidence in their own independence and autonomy.

› Talk to your Gen Y about the qualities of leadership that are important to your organization (for example, independent thinking,

Y in the Workplace

personal power with regard to problem-solving and decision-making, maturity, and emotional intelligence with regard to inter and intra-personal functioning) and have them set up goals to work on these qualities with your monitoring. Your monitoring consists of asking them about their progress and letting them continue to refine their goals as they continue to grow in these leadership areas.

> If a Generation Y employee's parent adds their input when there is a problem, set up a meeting with your Generation Y employee to discuss this issue. Talk to your Gen Y employee about the importance of handling their own problems explaining that, "This is your job—your life and your name is being signed to your work." Discuss what you expect from them and help them independently discover the steps they need to get there, including developing more independence and personal power with regard to their decision-making and problem solving. In addition, discuss the importance of reputation building within organizations and how it directly impacts promotion, increased responsibility, and relationships.

> Do not allow your Gen Y employee to treat you like a peer (with disrespect) or like their parent (with dependence). Again, make your expectations clear and point out concerns, in a supportive and emotionally intelligent manner, when they exist. If you are shocked by certain behaviors then speak up. This will enhance the lines of communication and will create a mature work relationship, while also modeling for a Gen Y employee what appropriate and successful work relationships look like.

Why it works

Let's face it: The behaviors that have been described throughout this chapter simply do not fly in corporations. Not only are they disruptive, the behaviors prevent growth and sour reputations. Many behaviors are those that organizations should not tolerate. Encouraging your Gen Y employee to develop their own parachutes and enhance their personal power by gaining appropriate independence from their parents, especially when it comes to the workplace, only enhances the relationship you will be able to form with your employee and their own ability to succeed in the workplace.

70

Idea into action

Emily Scherberth, owner and Chief Connections Officer of Symphony PR & Marketing, shared a story with us that we feel is a great example of how to help Generation Y utilize their parachutes: "I noticed that many of my entry level supervisees were often anxious and heavily dependent on feedback, so I started meeting with each of them individually on a monthly basis where they would tell me what their goals were and then outline how they were going to work on those goals throughout the next month. Sometimes their goals were not directly work related, such as wanting to get along better with a coworker. However, they independently chose their goals. I simply did my best to guide them and let them do the problem-solving independently. Then during monthly meeting updates, I would hold them accountable for both their progress and lack of progress."

Coaching solutions simplified

Coaching Solution 1

Title: Friend and family day.

Purpose: To create opportunities to learn more about your employees and the important people in their life.

Outcome: Relationship building, improved trust, investment in your employees, enhanced work-life fluidity.

Coaching Solution 2

Title: Be there and go there.

Purpose: To build, understand, and honor the importance of the supervisor-supervisee relationship.

Outcome: Increased alliance between supervisor and supervisee, improved work relationships, stronger loyalty, and increased trust.

Coaching Solution 3

Title: When it comes to families, beat 'em or join 'em.

Purpose: To communicate clear expectations, policies, and procedures about family involvement in the workplace.

Outcome: Boundary setting, awareness and clarity of expectations, and up-to-date policies.

Coaching Solution 4

Title: Helping Gen Y's pack their parachutes and make their own lunches.

Purpose: To help your Gen Y employee develop increased autonomy, responsibility, and accountability.

Outcome: Increased responsibility and accountability, personal, and professional development.

——Chapter 4——

Gold Stars for Everyone: Motivation and Generation Y

"Motivation is a fire from within. If someone else tries to light that fire under you, chances are it will burn very briefly."
—Stephen R. Convey, author of *7 Habits of Highly Effective People*

"Luke was an amazing employee. He went from an entry-level position to an account executive within a year. It was fast, but he was talented and we wanted him to have the acknowledgment he deserved. While working with Luke and other Gen Y's, I quickly realized how important it was for them to receive praise and rewards, so I created the 'Wall of Fame' where every week someone would get their work acknowledged publicly on the wall. I also held monthly individualized coaching meetings with them to help them work on their identified goals. Our Gen Y's don't realize what an amazing company they work for, because they haven't worked for other companies. We have an incredibly supportive work environment, but I've seen junior staff leave for greater tangible rewards. In fact, when Luke earned his last promotion the raise he was given was less than expected due to worries the company had about the economy. However, it was still a 4 percent raise with an additional spot bonus. It was explained to Luke that the raise was not performance driven, but rather economically driven. This was not enough for Luke, and despite the fact that he had a tremendous amount of respect from the upper management, a great working relationship with our clients, and worked in a supportive environment where he

> *could basically spend time the way he wished, he gave it up to work for another company with a well-known reputation of being a difficult place to work and having unhappy employees. He left our company for a company that could offer him higher tangible rewards. He didn't realize when he left that money isn't everything. I guess the other fulfilling parts of a job didn't matter to him, only the reward."*
>
> *Emily Scherberth, owner and chief connections officer,*
> *Symphony PR & Marketing*

We are constantly dancing between internal and external motivation in our daily lives. Sometimes we all need a little ego rubbing to keep us going and sometimes we just do it because it fits our character, our personal mission, and our vision of how we want to live our lives. This is true of all generations. However, there is a shift occurring in the social landscape of today's new generation of workers. More specifically, Generation Y thrives on external reward and praise, and they are driven more by external motivation than they are by internal motivation. This has affected the work environment. They are a generation that seeks instant gratification rather than long-term investments when it comes to work. There are complaints that are heard across organizations about Gen Y's need for external reinforcement and rewards to be motivated to excel (for example, bonuses, praise, recognition, salary increases, work-from-home-days, special privileges, gifts, and added benefits).

This chapter focuses on Generation Y's tendency to be externally motivated, what happens in the workplace when external motivation is the driving force, and how to coach and manage your externally motivated employees more effectively while assisting Generation Y to become more internally motivated. By coaching this generation to be driven more by internal motivation, you will be increasing their ability to be successful, productive, independent, and self-reliant, and decreasing their reliance on your time for personalized individual attention and feedback.

Back to the (psychological) basics

A motivational shift has occurred in the workplace: from internal to external

It is important to look beyond the behavior and understand what drives your employees, so that you can be effective at motivating and influencing them. Are you finding that you are having more difficulty understanding what is behind Generation Y's behavior? Not surprising. As a whole, Generation Y is at the extreme end of external motivation when compared to other generations. It is not that other generations are not externally motivated; we all are in some situations. It is just that this generation is so large in size and has such a strong voice that their preferences tend to be seen as excessive. Their external motivation needs are clear. So what is the difference between external and internal motivation?

External (extrinsic) motivation is when someone is motivated to engage in a task for the purpose of being recognized and rewarded, or because they fear punishment or consequence. When someone is externally motivated they seek tangible rewards, look for praise from others, expect immediate feedback for their work, and demand acknowledgement for their "great" work after each step. The externally motivated salaried employee would stay late to work on a project because his or her boss is also staying late, and they will be recognized for their extra work. Externally motivated employees often feel they have little control over what happens to them and their environment, and they often feel that the possibility of change is out of their personal control. This is a problem in the workplace because an individual who is externally motivated and is not receiving consistent external rewards will easily be distracted from the task due to insecurity and frustration and subsequently, performance can decrease.

On the other hand, when one experiences internal (intrinsic) motivation, they are doing a task because they are motivated from within and feel fulfillment from the act of engaging in the task. External rewards are appreciated; however, they are not the reason why the internally motivated individual chooses to engage in a task. An example of internal motivation in the workplace is someone who is salaried but works overtime without compensation because they are committed to their idea. They continue working to contribute, not necessarily to be noticed. This is the employee who may be working on their ideas while they are running on the treadmill, getting a shower in the morning, or staying late at work because they just have to finish the project before they consider their work day finished. These employees often feel they have control over what happens to them and feel they have the ability to make changes when necessary. Being internally motivated in the workplace is a desired quality, because tasks are accomplished regardless of reward and recognition; they are accomplished because there is internal pride and motivation to succeed.

Shrinkwrapped

Psychologist Julian Rotter discussed internal and external motivation as a part of his Locus of Control theory. In response to the question, "Why did something happen?" people with an internal locus of control believe that they control why it happened, have control over making changes, and that valued experience occurs while doing the task. Individuals with an external locus of control believe that the event, and the change that needs to happen, is outside of their control. These individuals will persist with the task as long as the external motivator is present.

A good example highlighting the difference between internal and external motivation came from a HR executive named Helen. Helen is responsible for leading initiatives to train and motivate the company's employees in order to build a cohesive, responsible, and energetic staff. She has been with this company for approximately 25 years and has truly been challenged by how much more creative she has had to become to engage and motivate her company's younger employees (for example, prizes and gifts). As a Boomer executive, she has found it difficult to rationalize the effort it takes to motivate her younger staff, but feels stuck because traditionally the company has recruited newly degreed individuals sprinkled with the occasional seasoned researchers.

"We hire researchers who are new graduates for research positions within our company. They have achieved the highest level of education in their field and due to demand they have many opportunities for employment. They also receive a high level of compensation without any real world work experience. They truly feel entitled just because they have finished their degree. It takes us four weeks to train them and almost six months of experience before they are really up and running. They want lunches, gifts, prizes, advancements, and acknowledgment for everything that they do and feel it should be part of the job. We find that when these aspects are not incorporated, they slack off a bit. This is compared to our other new hires that are seasoned in the field and have transferred from other companies. They tend to come to work for us because of our reputation and because they believe in our mission and vision.

Helen, HR executive,
Marketing Research Company

The underpinnings of Generation Y's tendency toward external motivation

Generation Y's ability to be internally motivated has been negatively influenced by the self-inflation movement. Gen Y's were raised on a healthy dose of accolades and praise at home, at school, and within their communities where rewards and a sense of excelling, often without real work or reason, were the focus rather than constructive criticism and learning how to be a good loser. Never "losing" means never learning from mistakes, and, therefore, there tends to be a lack of the development of an internal drive based on a need/desire to improve. Without failing from time to time, how can one learn to do better? Or learn what one is truly good at doing?

Did this really happen? Yes!

"When I first started teaching, martial arts competitions were between 25 students and there were awards given to the first, second, and third place winners. During the childhoods of Generation Y, fourth, fifth, and sixth places were added with competitions broken into smaller groups (as little as four) so everyone could win a prize. In addition, the pressure from parents caused martial arts schools to add different levels to each belt color so children wouldn't have to wait to place with a higher belt. Also, everyone would get a ribbon for showing up. Kids began running up and asking for their ribbon and they hadn't even done anything yet. A quote I frequently hear is 'half of success is just showing up.' What? This just teaches getting something without having to achieve anything. We have created a generation where we have changed the standards rather than changing the person to meet the standards."

Stevie Ray, executive director,

Stevie Ray's Improv Company

Overall, Generation Y grew up with the idea that no matter what they do, they are important and should receive recognition and/or reward regardless of their behavior. When you are constantly rewarded and praised for lack of performance or subpar performance, you start developing strong expectations for reward and recognition for everything that you do. These expectations just get stronger and stronger with age if they are not corrected. However, because of the self-inflation movement, there is a general consensus among this generation that they are internally motivated and driven to succeed. This occurred because throughout their lives up until entering the workforce they have been given rewards and accolades for their performance regardless of success and have developed a belief in themselves that even minimal effort and subpar results are adequate. This has shaped their standard of excellence. They believe that they are driven and working within their own internally motivated standards. However, that is not a reality that they share with others generations. This reflects a lack of self-awareness when it comes to motivational needs.

Therefore, what we are seeing is a generation that has a strong need for external motivation disguised as a false sense of internal motivation. With this generational shift, while some behaviors may appear to be the result of internal motivation, it is actually inspired by external rewards and recognition. The problem with this shell of a belief in one's own motivation and ability, which has been observed in college classes and later in the workplace, is that it can crack easily if challenged.

External motivation into adulthood

One sign of maturity is being able to delay gratification and find internal motivation and pride to succeed and do well. As previously stated, the disservice of constant kudos and praise regardless of accomplishment has created a false sense of internal motivation and a need for constant external motivation. In response, managers seem to be constantly complaining these days about how difficult it is to engage and retain their Gen Y employees, and also how difficult it is to give them honest feedback and constructive criticism without them falling to pieces or leaving the company. Managers have complained that the time required meeting these needs, the constant interruptions and need for personal attention, and finding creative ways to reward this generation has been quite challenging. This can create more work, more stress, and more gray hairs in the process. The catch-22 is that without the personal attention, constant praise and creative strategies to satisfy external motivation, productivity and commitment suffers.

Did this really happen? Yes!

"I gave instructions for a task and left the office for a few hours. When I returned I found my Gen Y employee on a social networking site chatting with friends. I assumed he was finished with the task, so I asked him for it. He replied, "Oh, I was stuck on how to do this part of it so I was waiting until you returned to ask you how to proceed." I asked him why he didn't call to ask me and he replied that he hadn't thought about it, but he didn't want to continue until I told him what to do next."

Stevie Ray, executive director

The problem with external motivation is that through time, if behavior that was internally motivated becomes externally motivated, the intrinsic motivation disappears. So if an employee likes getting into work early because they are internally motivated to have extra time to work on an aspect of a project they like, but then start getting externally rewarded for coming in early for a few months, when the extra money for coming in early is withdrawn, so too is their motivation for coming in early. Intrinsic motivation can be easily replaced by extrinsic motivation. Additionally, futilely showering external rewards on someone who lacks internal motivation will not inspire that missing quality. It just might cause an extra emphasis on their expectation or dependence on outside rewards. Here is a good example of how external rewards can change internal motivation.

Tamika Johnson loves the practice of law. During her first year of practicing, Tamika worked for a not-for-profit organization providing legal services to abused women and children. She worked long hours for little pay. The nonprofit organization lost their funding and she obtained a position as an attorney at a large, profitable law firm. In her new company, the emphasis is on external rewards. During the past year, she has found that she is looking more for how much of a bonus she is going to get on a case rather than focusing on the excitement and challenge of the case. For Tamika, the external reward focus on money, bonuses, and elite lunching has replaced her passion and focus on practicing law for the sake of practicing law.

How it plays out in the workplace: three advantages of external motivation

"As much as they may need their morning coffee to get up to speed each day, Generation Y employees—those workers between ages 21 and 30—need their bosses' praise and recognition to stay motivated in their jobs."
—Kathy Gurchiek, associate editor for HR News, SHRM

Working with thoughts of "what will my boss think?"

Although external motivation includes bonuses such as time off, promotions, and money, Generation Y's most sought after reward lies with what their boss thinks of their performance. You would be hard pressed to find a boss who would not like an employee to work with thoughts of pleasing them. What a nice way to function as a boss when you know your Gen Y employees are motivated by "What will my boss think?" In its ideal form, this company experience would result in cohesion between what the boss expects and the hard work that the Gen Y employee will engage in to please their boss. The desire for receiving praise to an extent never seen before in other generations comes from their tendency to be motivated extrinsically.

A Gen Y says:

Gen Y employees talk about how important it is for bosses to take the mentoring role and guide them with their work. Although at times this can be annoying to managers and supervisors, Gen Y employees say they really value this feedback loop and that it helps them stay motivated and committed.

Natural team players

Generation Y tends to work well in teams. They are interested in what others think and say about them, as well as focused on coming to a solution where everyone agrees. Team environments breed opportunities for team members to encourage each other, hold each other accountable, and recognize individual contributions. Gen Y's tendency to care about what others think creates an amazing impetus for strong team work, and encouragement for individual and team contributions. Teams operate well when they are recognized for their contributions and when individual team members are held accountable for their work, but for Gen Y this might be only when they do a good job. Because Gen Y thrives off of recognition, encouragement, and praise, they operate well in a team environment.

A leader says:

"The Ys are a generation that prefers to collaborate and work in teams. Constant communication, connection and kudos have always been a part of their lives."
Angelo Anastasio, CEO,
Greenable

As long as you know what I need, we are all happy!

Would you like to make more money? Have more time off? Wear your jeans to work on a Friday? Gen Y's would not only prefer these rewards, but they actually expect and demand them. They have always been rewarded for their behavior, whether warranted or not, and they have often received these rewards immediately. If the companies they work for do not provide their desired rewards on a consistent basis, they often become disappointed and insecure, ultimately leading to low productivity. Although this may seem like a problem, it can be used to a company's advantage; straightforward extrinsic plans for external compensation can be put into place in a way that motivates Gen Y's, such as weekly pats on the back and pizza days. Although this generation needs to develop internal motivation, in the meantime, knowing that they tend to be externally motivated makes it easy for companies to engage and motivate them. However, this should not be the only way you are motivating them; this might exacerbate their need for external rewards and ultimately create more stress on managers. In addition, it will most likely have an impact on the loyalty of your Gen Y employees. Truth be told, Gen Y is more likely to leave a job if they are not externally rewarded. Everyone loves pizza, dress-down Fridays, and rewards. Gen Y just speaks up about it. Everyone wants it equally but the other generations will not necessarily job hop because of it—a Gen Y might.

A leader says:

"We incorporate money in our budget in order to give spot bonuses for great work in increments of $100, $200, and $500. This is far more motivating than just saying, 'You're doing great work.'"

Kevin Mercuri, president,

Propheta Communications

How it plays out in the workplace: three challenges of external motivation

"It is up to us to give ourselves recognition. If we wait for it to come from others, we feel resentful when it doesn't, and when it does, we may well reject it."

—Spencer Tracy (1900–1967)

> *"Last summer we thought of a creative way to reward our staff and we decided to buy an ocean-side house in a popular beach area. No one even blinked an eye. Twenty-five-year old account executives getting full use of a five-bedroom home in the Hamptons for the weekend and no one blinked an eye. They expected it, saw it as a given. They feel that everyone is entitled to rewards like this even if they are a mediocre employee."*
> Kevin Mercuri, president,
> Propheta Communications

The crack in the shell of Gen Y's internal motivation

Being externally motivated with a false sense of internal motivation can have serious consequences for some Gen Ys and the companies they work for. Gen Ys have successfully learned that they are important and that they can succeed and harness their strengths to accomplish all that they can. However, being raised on a toxic message of "we all are winners" ultimately makes real-world losses (and they will and do occur) extremely difficult and wounding. When this shell of being motivated externally is shattered with a workplace comment of constructive criticism, rather than incorporating the criticism and making improvements, it is frequently damaging. This can be devastating and paralyzing to the Gen Y employee, thereby negatively affecting the workforce. This is often surprising to an unsuspecting manager issuing what they think of as straightforward recommendations and/or job demands. For example, when did the simple managerial request of, "Make sure you tell someone when you go to lunch so we know you're out," have such a dramatic impact? Welcome to the art of managing Generation Y. The following story is from a multi-media Generation Y business owner who relayed his frustration with this generation when giving constructive criticism.

> **A leader says:**
> *"When I accepted this management role as art director, I definitely thought that I would have an easier time managing my Gen Y cohorts since I'm one of them. However, I have had a tremendous amount of difficulty giving my Gen Y employees feedback, which is an essential skill to develop, especially as a graphic artist. I have found that when I give constructive*

criticism or client feedback that they do not agree with many of them are sensitive. I've also found that they rely on me to give them a lot of praise and pats on the back, even when it's not really deserved. This has definitely been my biggest struggle as a manager because I'm a pretty young art director, and didn't react like this when I was in lower positions."
J.D. Haldin, art director,
Software Development and Web Design Company

If you tell me how great I am, I'll continue to do my excellent work and continue to work here

If one is motivated by the recognition and rewards others provide, then one will be extremely disappointed and disgruntled if the managers in an organization do not have the time, energy, or interest in providing it on a regular basis. Managers, HR professionals, and organizations are faced with the challenge of engaging Gen Y quickly and consistently through creative and direct ways of reward and motivation. Y's need for encouragement, praise, and rewards to get moving can be exhausting and time consuming, making it difficult for others to accomplish their own tasks and goals. Praise and recognition for Gen Y are necessary for motivation to occur, and this can lead to a higher level of productivity and loyalty.

One of the consequences of perceived inconsistent and delayed praise and recognition in the workforce is a generation of individuals who demonstrate little workplace loyalty with frequent job hopping due to serial disenchantment and disappointment. Lack of loyalty and productivity can have a devastating impact on the bottom line of companies not only because of the need for adaptive and flexible managers, HR professionals, and organizations, but also because of the financial impact of recruiting, training, and replacing job-hopping Y's.

Did this really happen? Yes!
A Gen X, Ethan, told us recently that one of his Gen Y coworkers said the following to him: "I'm really worried that I'm going to get fired. My boss didn't say anything to me today."

Why can't I Google to find the answer to whether or not my boss thinks I'm doing a good job?

This generation is equipped with so many technological resources that for Gen Y's it is old fashioned to question something without being able to find the answer immediately. When a question arises the answer is as simple as a keystroke away. Because Generation Y is so desperately in need of extrinsic motivation/external rewards to shine, the lack thereof can be damaging to their self-confidence, and, therefore, damaging to their motivation and commitment. When they are lifted up and praised, their talents can illuminate an organization and their commitment to the organization can be strengthened. However, when they are neglected in this area (or treated like other employees) their talents can be thwarted, ultimately impacting the organization's bottom line and their own personal potentials. Generation Y prefers this feedback immediately and also prefers to have feedback given consistently throughout the course of a project. This need for continual feedback prevents the development of patience, independent thinking, and the ability to delay gratification.

A leader says:

"They (Gen Y) want me to say 'good job,' 'great work,' 'you're amazing!' They want me to pump them up every day."
Claudia Ross, owner,
Cross Marketing

The takeaways so far...

If you remember nothing else, take away the following:

> Look beyond behavior and understand the drive.
> This is the generation who thrives off of external motivation. This results in the need for praise, tangible rewards, expectation for immediate feedback, and demand for constant acknowledgement from their supervisors and companies.
> The development of internal motivation is important to increase Gen Y's success in the workplace by decreasing their reliance on management's time to satisfy their need for personalized individual

attention and feedback. Developing internal motivation will increase their independence, self-reliance, and success.

›　You can use Gen Y's external motivation to your advantage by:

    ›　Defining your expectations clearly.

    ›　Using teams when appropriate.

    ›　Understanding their expectations.

›　Watch out for Gen Y's tendency to:

    ›　Show extreme and unexpected sensitivity when receiving constructive criticism and when perceiving failure.

    ›　Have continual need for feedback and external rewards.

    ›　Demand instant reward and gratification.

Now it's time to take some action. Here are the coaching solutions that we recommend to enhance the positives and manage the negatives when it comes to Gen Y and motivation.

Coaching solutions: building on strengths and addressing the challenges

When coaching a Generation Y employee, it is imperative to focus on how their unique characteristics, can serve as strengths in the workplace. Because Generation Y can have a false sense of internal motivation (which was developed and then continually rewarded externally), a problem occurs when the external motivation and rewards are not present or available immediately. For example, consider the employee who feels that rewards and acknowledgment should be daily parts of their job. Without these rewards they feel cheated, and subsequently performance plummets and morale sours. Sound familiar? Gen Y's tendency toward external motivation has created unique challenges for managers and HR professionals alike when it comes to grooming this generation and helping them become more self sufficient and committed in the workplace. Solutions are also offered to counteract Generation Y employees' need for external motivation while increasing their abilities to integrate the values and benefits of internal motivation within the workplace.

No-brainer coaching solutions

CS1: The 5-minute chat: rewards and team benefits

Take five minutes to meet with each employee to ask them their ideas about what would be extrinsically validating for the company culture as a whole, and your team specifically. If you are too busy to find the five minutes for each employee or you supervise a large group of people, you can create an e-mail or provide a paper questionnaire that they answer at the beginning or end of a meeting. Better yet, put this as an agenda item on your next team/department meeting, so that your staff can brainstorm together. Not only will you get the feedback you need, but you will be creating a team building opportunity. Here's an example of how to open this discussion:

> *"I would like to work toward creating opportunities for our team/our group to enhance our culture and have a little fun. When a project is completed, what three things could we do as a team/group to demonstrate our appreciation for a job well done? Also, what three things could I do as your manager/supervisor to reward you and show you my appreciation?"*

Important note: If there are certain policies in your company about time off and monetary compensation, you may want to define the boundaries of the rewards by stating, "please provide examples of non-monetary and non-schedule related rewards."

Why it works

This exercise in itself can be rewarding as it demonstrates, not only to Generation Y employees, but also to all of your employees, an interest and priority in the shared community and culture of your team. This conversation will probably be pleasantly surprising to many of your employees, because it provides them with an opportunity to express how they would like to be rewarded. This exercise also promotes an atmosphere of appreciation, because employee's needs are being addressed.

Idea into action

In a recent coaching session with a director of quality and affordability programs for a large managed care company, Dr. Lipkin made this recommendation after her client expressed frustration about engaging her younger team members with regard to team cohesiveness, low morale, and general burn out and motivation issues. This client chose to have individual meetings with her team, because her team was relatively small and manageable. She reported back that not only did she receive novel ideas about how she could motivate her staff, but many expressed appreciation that she had interest. In fact, Dr. Lipkin's client discussed the outcome of this strategy during one of her director meetings, and many of her colleagues followed suit and received positive outcomes.

CS2: The self-monitoring exercise

In order to help your Generation Y employees increase their self-awareness and begin taking ownership for their actions, help them begin to appreciate the importance of learning from their mistakes. Helping your Gen Y employees increase their self-awareness and take ownership requires the following steps:

1. Begin with an evaluation and an understanding of where you believe your Gen Y's need to increase their ability to independently monitor themselves and take ownership for their behaviors to ultimately improve their potential of success. Some common areas of improvement that managers talk about with regard to their Gen Y employees include: being too bold, always asking "why" something needs to be completed or finished in a certain way, spending a lot of time on the Internet on non-work related websites, feeling that a task is "below them," not understanding how their behavior impacts everyone else around them, and so on.

2. Once you have completed your evaluation and have identified the behavior that you would like to work on with your Gen Y employee, you will want to meet with them to give them your observations and good, clear examples (coupled with clear expectations of change and growth) of these behaviors in action.

   Note: Be prepared for resistance when you identify a "problem area," because as a whole, this generation has trouble hearing constructive criticism. When a Gen Y employee demonstrates resistance, refer to Coaching Solution 2 entitled "The Ice Cream Sandwich" in Chapter 2 to help present the feedback.

3. Once you have made them aware of these behaviors, give them some time to see if they see those same behaviors as well. Then set up another meeting and design a plan of attack where they begin monitoring their own behavior and comparing their own behavior with the norms established by the company or team.

For example, if an employee is frequently late, help them track their lateness by doing it for them first (this is your concrete evidence that this is a behavior that is in need of change), then have them track it for a week and judge their behavior in comparison with other employees (is everyone coming in late?). Then have them take time to brainstorm why they are coming in late and what benefits may occur if they change this behavior. In addition, have them brainstorm how they can reward themselves for regulating the target behavior(s). Note that the change in behavior will be gradual. In addition, although time is being taken away from other responsibilities, it will be recouped by sustained behavioral change and productivity in your Gen Y employee.

Why it works

This coaching solution works by assisting your Gen Y employee to begin to self-critique by hearing it from you first, seeing it for themselves by monitoring their behaviors, and then setting up their own individual self-reward system. This solution is similar to a food or exercise journal in the sense that it makes you conscious of your behavior and choices, as long as you are honest about it. This task helps your Gen Y employees develop accountability for their behavior, heightens awareness of the impact of their actions on others, and ultimately helps shape preferred behavior in the workplace.

Idea into action

Glenn Reynolds, a team leader at a managed care company, was in charge of overseeing his team's day-to-day activities and productivity. Most of his team was fairly young, ranging in ages from 22 to 29 years old. His team's hours were from 8:30 a.m. to 5:30 p.m., Monday through Friday with no overtime. One of his team members, Lindsay (25 years old), consistently came in 15–20 minutes late at least four out of five days a week. Because the team was on a rotation schedule with regard to breaks, Lindsay's lateness would often interfere with scheduling, case assignments, and breaks throughout the days. Lindsay would always apologize for being late and was very creative with her excuses, but everyone on the team was impacted and upset by her negligence. Glenn decided to implement the self-monitoring exercise. He suggested that Lindsay keep a record on a piece of paper when she "clocks in" everyday. Because she was coming in late, Glenn decided that he would keep a record of everyone else's arrival to compare to Lindsey's arrival times; however, Glenn made the request that Lindsey note down on her list everyone who was already there and working by the time she arrived each day. Lindsay and Glenn agreed that they would meet in one week to review the findings. By the end of the week, Glenn noticed that Lindsey improved her attendance. During their meeting the following week, Glenn reviewed Lindsey's record and they had a discussion about her arrival to work. Lindsey commented on her awareness of her lateness and the embarrassment she felt toward the end of the week. She also started noticing the irritation that others were feeling about her lateness. They discussed this, and from that point on, the number of times she was late did not come to a screeching halt, but they reduced significantly and her awareness of her behaviors and the impact of these behaviors increased drastically.

Brainer coaching solutions

CS3: Self-protective advising system

The constant need for praise and acknowledgment can be time consuming and cause significant interference for a busy manager/supervisor of a Generation Y employee. We suggest creating an advising system and teaming Generation Y employees with employees from other generations to allow for another layer of feedback, and also to help team members learn about each other rather than relying on assumptions and ignorance. When people know each other on a personal, caring level, feedback is not only productive and meaningful, but it also prevents empty complaining and negativity (that is, broad assumptions about a person based on a generation or stereotype). However, this needs to be undertaken with care, as in the beginning there will probably be apprehension based on generalizations that each generation has about the other.

Why it works

Using this advising system not only allows for a buffer for the constant "looking to the boss" for feedback and praise, but also provides for deeper, more understanding relationships between coworkers. It also allows for an opportunity to provide for genuine feedback from advisors to Gen Y employees based on real knowledge of personal attributes, areas of excellence at work, and personal weakness within the workplace. This will ultimately decrease external motivation and increase internal motivation, because feedback will be genuine based on real work interactions and experiences.

Idea into action

Ten years ago, Dr. Perrymore remembers the confusion of starting her new position as a professor, and fondly recalls being linked with an advisor through the college's volunteer mentoring program. It was invaluable to be able to learn about the college through a seasoned professor who was willing to take time out of his busy schedule to serve as a support. This helped her understand her role as an adjunct professor, and understand the ropes of the tenure process a few years later. What she noticed most of all was that while there were age differences between the new professors called "junior faculty" (who were mostly younger and inexperienced) and the "senior faculty," the mentoring program began to integrate younger and older faculty members who eventually developed mutual respect and often became friends and trusted colleagues. After a few years, she thought that she would incorporate this program with incoming freshman psychology majors and volunteer senior psychology majors. Success! A success that can be used in companies with their newest and youngest employees to offer another layer of support, an additional source for feedback, and possibly help bridge the generational gap.

CS4: Recognizing and harnessing strengths exercise

When a Generation Y employee first comes on board, it would be beneficial to find out about their strengths. Not only will this clue you into your new employee's unique talents, but it will also force your new employee to take the time to think about what genuinely makes him/her shine. Your Gen Y employee will have the opportunity to reflect on what they believe their strengths are and receive genuine feedback. This assists Generation Y with understanding their talents instead of asking others to tell them their strengths through constant praise seeking behaviors.

To help complete this task, you may want to ask your Generation Y employee the following series of questions:

1. Tell me about a peak experience that you had in your life either personally or professionally. This experience should reflect a time when you felt most alive and most united with something you have done or were a part of.

2. Based on this peak experience, what strengths did you learn that you possessed?

3. How do you think those strengths can be applied to your new role?

4. How can I help you realize those strengths on a daily basis?

This exercise is based on the theory of Appreciative Inquiry (AI), and can be done in a one-on-one meeting or used as a technique with an existing team when team building is needed. When using this exercise to increase cohesiveness in a team, it is best to hire an outside facilitator skilled in the use of AI techniques to help develop and strengthen teams. In addition, it is a great technique to use during a new hire orientation. Not only will this task heighten awareness of your new employee's individual, genuine talents, it will strengthen feelings of appreciation, loyalty, and productivity within the team due to the recognition of their skills and talents.

Shrinkwrapped

Appreciative Inquiry (AI) is a organizational development process created veloped by David Cooperrider that focuses on positive change and renewed performance by identifying what works in an organization rather than what does not work. This process can also be applied to individuals. It is a strategy that requires a particular way of asking questions that helps an organization, team, or individual imagine how they are going to function using their strengths to achieve optimal and preferred organizational or personal effectiveness. When this is identified and believed, an organization, team, or person can thrive and move toward their envisioned future.

Why it works

Taking time to get to know how people shine is one of the most important aspects of being a supervisor or a manager. When you commit this time and energy to an individual or group of individuals, you give them the impression that learning about them is important. You also have the potential to inspire people to understand and live up to the standards/strengths that they have set for themselves and help them to realize their genuine areas of strength for the work that they do. In addition, this process feels empowering and inspiring, which boosts morale. One of the results is that it tends to align people's individual goals with the organizational goals. The added bonus to this task is that loyalty naturally deepens when you recognize and work within people's talents and strengths.

Important note: If you are a manager or supervisor who will be conducting this AI strategy, it is recommended that you be brought through this process first. Understanding the personal impact that it has is important. This will help you be authentic when helping others to realize their strengths.

Idea into action

Dr. Lipkin ran a team-building retreat for a company that had team members in two different states. She was called in to do this retreat after the team grew significantly in size and after many unfavorable policy changes were implemented. On a whole, they were all feeling overworked, underappreciated, and very dissatisfied with their work/life balance. The team was a multi-generational team, which was also causing tension. Dr. Lipkin conducted individual interviews with each team member prior to the team retreat. She found out that every team member was struggling to understand what was expected of them and everyone had a different idea of the goals for the overall team. Tensions were high and there was an extreme amount of resentment, mostly because of not knowing one another due to the two different locations, and because work was interfering with their personal lives. Dr. Lipkin used the retreat to conduct an appreciative inquiry team-building process. The first part focused on helping each team member identify his or her strengths, talents, and preferred futures (goals) through self-reflection and interviewing. The second part involved identifying the strengths of the team and the overall mission and purpose of their work through group brainstorming and small group break-outs. By the end of the retreat, there were several optimal results:

1. The team was on the same page about the purpose of the work.

2. Each team member reported a significant change regarding his or her level of empowerment and connection to his or her own talents.

3. There was an enhanced appreciation and new understanding of each team member's talents.

4. There was a significant positive change with regard to team cohesiveness.

5. Each team member committed to changing his or her work environment to support his or her strengths by addressing the barriers that existed within the team.

Big-brainer coaching solutions

CS5: The crescendo: incremental promotions

Gen Y tends to have unrealistic expectations of taking over the world. Okay, actually their expectations usually surround taking over, or gaining a high-level position, in the companies for which they work after the first few months of employment. Although they may be talented, we all know that this is not always realistic. However, this quality or expectation is not going to change. It is part of their internal workings, which is much more powerful than any reality check you may offer them when you say no. So, we recommend honoring their expectations by providing what we call The Crescendo. More specifically, from the very beginning, when you identify a quality, hardworking Gen Y employee who will eventually earn a promotion, set in place different levels of responsibilities associated with their job description. Have them start with the first level of responsibilities, and as they demonstrate that they are able to handle more via quality, responsible work, add the next set of responsibilities. Of course this should come hand-in-hand with some form of compensation, whether it be in the form of recognition, title enhancement (for example, junior to senior), or monetary compensation.

Why it works

This works because this is what this generation was used to when they were growing up in school and in their extracurricular activities. Every task had different steps, and every step of the way was honored and rewarded. Rather than fighting what they know, work within what they are used to in order to help manage their expectations and prevent complaints of boredom, feeling undervalued, and ultimately lack of loyalty.

CS6: The new world token economy: teaching delayed gratification

Generation Y employees have a difficult time delaying gratification and instead seek praise and reward immediately. They are wearing on their bosses by seeking this reinforcement on what may appear to be an inconsistent basis, at inopportune times, or all the time. In order to prevent burnout and frustration for all involved parties, create a reward and recognition system similar to that of the token economy.

Shrinkwrapped

A token economy is a form of behavior modification based on B.F. Skinner's work, designed to increase wanted behavior and decrease unwanted behavior with the use of rewards (tokens). Individuals receive tokens immediately after displaying wanted behavior. The tokens are collected and later exchanged for something meaningful to the person. Ultimately, this will result in a consistent display of the preferred behavior.

If using token economies in the traditional manner within the workplace, then a program would be implemented where tokens are given to employees who showed up to work on time, dressed appropriately, had excellent attendance for a month, and so on. Then these tokens could be saved up and "spent" on desired rewards. For example, work from home days, longer lunch hour on a given day, extra vacation days, dress-down day, bring your dog to work for the day, and so on. However, implementing a token economy for basic, expected behaviors in the workplace (showing up for work) would be absolutely ridiculous and demeaning.

So, here's our spin on the "token economy" in the workplace. It has an emphasis on chunking tasks and then positively reinforcing the individual or team after the chunked task is completed. The goal is to help your Gen Y employees lessen their need for continual external motivation (coming in the form of praise and reward) by helping them develop skills with regard to delayed gratification. How do you do this? Basically, develop benchmarks (that is, tasks chunked together) throughout the course of a project. Make these benchmarks clear to the whole team, so that it is very apparent as to when evaluation, praise, and reward will occur. If a team member seeks out kudos prior to the scheduled benchmark/token time they should be redirected to the agreed upon plan of action. It is important to note that this is different than feedback given to help a team member understand the direction or scope of a project. If the team accomplishes the group of tasks that are chunked together then follow through with the action plan of reward and praise.

Why it works

When we group similar tasks together, the tasks appear easier and more manageable to accomplish. By creating reward benchmarks at the end of each group of tasks, motivation for reward will be deferred, and you will help your Gen Y employees internalize the concept of delayed gratification.

Important note: As with any behavioral change (whether you are teaching a dog how to sit, a child how to follow classroom rules, or an employee how you expect work to be completed) being consistent is imperative. Also, when rules change, typically there is an increase in the undesired behavior at first. Therefore, the first few times this approach is used many Gen Y's may look even more intensely for feedback, and will need to be refocused back to the plan of the project and gently reminded when feedback will be provided. It is important that the manager in charge of the project does not offer feedback and/or reward until the time specified in the token plan.

Idea into action

A company was having difficulty with the Gen Y employees in their education and training department due to their constant need for reinforcement for their work. This was interfering with manager time and productivity. In the application of the new world token economy with this team, the following behaviors were addressed:

Unwanted Behavior = Constant interruptions for reinforcement

Wanted Behavior = Delayed gratification for reinforcement

Goal = More productivity and less demands on manager time

Here's what happened: There were three Gen Y employees in the education and training department. In applying the token economy, the manager decided to have these three employees create a five-day national training program together. When they started working on the project, the manager of this team was constantly bombarded with requests for review and pats on the back before they would continue working. These interruptions became so frequent that the manager decided to implement a "New World Token Economy System." He took the original outline of the training curriculum and divided it into 10 equal parts. He then met with his team and told them that in order to help them to do their best work he was going to help them organize the project into 10 parts (chunked tasks). He scheduled 10 different meetings throughout the course of four months in which they would come together as a team, review the part they had worked on, and celebrate their progress. At the beginning of this "experiment," it was difficult for the manager to stop their habit of interrupting him for praise and reinforcement. However, after the first two parts passed, he was able to successfully deflect their interruptions and remind them about their next scheduled meeting. By the end of the 10 parts/meetings, the three Gen Y employees were much less disruptive and needy, evidencing delayed gratification.

CS7: Quarterly review: treatment planning for businesses

Another way to counteract the need for continual praise and recognition is to build in informal quarterly progress reviews, which leads to the more formal annual review. Providing these quarterly progress reviews help to reduce the guessing game and subsequent harassing for praise. In addition, it may help Generation Y to internalize delayed gratification. Developing a system where employees are required to journal/blog non-immediate concerns, issues, and progress that can be shared in the review helps fulfill the Generation Y employee's need to communicate their successes. It also helps them begin to internalize completing tasks for the purpose of completing tasks, versus for the purpose of reward (internalization versus externalization). This quarterly process of performance review will also help, because there will be no surprises when you need to appraise them for compensation during annual formal reviews. It also allows you and your Gen Y employee to create an action plan for developmental areas that need to be addressed throughout the course of the year.

Important note: If you find that your Gen Y employees are working primarily toward quarterly goals and missing the bigger picture, be sure to incorporate Coaching Solution 5: The Integrated Development Plan from Chapter 6.

Why it works

This technique allows for structured and expected feedback, which is frequently demanded by Generation Y employees. The added benefit of this approach is that you are helping to develop your future leaders by providing them with subtle exercises in delayed gratification. In addition, this technique protects an organization with regard to retention and development by informally and incrementally redirecting and correcting Generation Y employees. It also protects the Generation Y employee's ego by avoiding annual "bombshells" during the yearly review, which could ultimately wound the Generation Y employee and reduce their productivity and effectiveness (for example, "Why didn't they tell me? I could've/would've done it differently. I thought I was doing great.")

Idea into action

A large financial institution was accustomed to doing yearly reviews. These reviews were very time consuming and often surprised employees, because this formal and comprehensive feedback was given so rarely. They decided to implement a pilot program in which quarterly reviews were conducted with their direct managers. The employees were told to keep a log about their performance, accomplishments, and concerns throughout the course of each quarter. At the end of the quarter, they were asked to fill out a short, open-ended questionnaire and schedule an appointment with their direct manager. During these meetings, their personal reflections and the manager's feedback were discussed. Goals were set in these meetings for the next quarter. Not only did this help employees feel heard and acknowledged for their work, it helped manage their expectations, set the action to correct problems and made the process of the comprehensive annual review much easier to do. Although it may appear that this was more time consuming, in actuality it was not, because it allowed the managers to gather data in increments and spread out their work through-out the year. In addition, the reviews were more honest and useful because they were correcting problems and reinforcing positive performance through-out the course of the year. The pilot program was implemented.

Coaching solutions simplified:

Coaching Solution 1

Title: The five-minute chat: rewards and team benefits.

Purpose: To find out what external motivations work best for your employees.

Outcome: Knowledge of the most effective external motivators for your employees, team building, and increased morale.

Coaching Solution 2

Title: The self-monitoring exercise.

Purpose: To hold your Gen Y employees accountable for their behavior, make them aware of how their behaviors impact others, and help them make appropriate changes.

Outcome: Self-awareness, increased accountability, ability to self-critique, and changed behavior.

Coaching Solution 3

Title: Self-protective advising system.

Purpose: To provide additional levels of feedback while decreasing reliance on boss for advice.

Outcome: Feedback from multiple sources, intergenerational relationship building, and increased support system.

Coaching Solution 4

Title: Recognizing and harnessing strengths exercise.

Purpose: To enhance self-reflection around strengths and to decrease reliance on others for feedback.

Outcome: Identification of one's talents, increased loyalty, and improved motivation to work on one's strengths.

Coaching Solution 5

Title: The crescendo: incremental promotions.

Purpose: To give your Gen Y increasingly more responsibility as they demonstrate quality work.

Outcome: Manage expectations for promotion and provide for incremental promotions/responsibility giving based on performance.

Coaching Solution 6

Title: The new world token economy: teaching delayed gratification.

Purpose: To increase wanted behaviors and decrease undesired behaviors with less reliance on the need for constant feedback.

Outcome: Reward and recognition system, behavioral change, and more self-reliance.

Coaching Solution 7

Title: Quarterly review: treatment planning for businesses.

Purpose: To provide more frequent review of employee performance to enhance understanding of strengths and weaknesses.

Outcome: Internalization of delayed gratification, increased knowledge regarding expectations and areas for improvement, and action planning for developmental areas.

──Chapter 5──

Talk 2 Me Instead of Texting Me: Communication and Generation Y

"Even if you do learn to speak correct English, whom are you going to speak it to?"
—Clarence Darrow (1857–1938)

> **"We have a student teacher in his 20s who just started in our school. His** *professionalism and sense of responsibility are very different from when I was student teaching. First, his cell phone rings in class, which is just great for student concentration. When asked to shut it off and keep it put away during school hours, he resisted and put it on vibrate, so he could check it during class—so inappropriate! He has already gone onto my computer, which is in the classroom, without my permission to do his banking and started saving files on my computer. I also had to talk with him about logging on to the computer throughout the day to check his social networking sites and e-mail. He actually has done this while the students are in the room! He has yet to show up the recommended 20 minutes before school starts to meet and discuss the plans for the day. I'm hoping this young man is one of a kind and does not reflect the attitudes of the next generation of teachers."*
>
> *Mrs. Todd, elementary school teacher,*
> *Massachusetts Public School System*

Julian, a director of sales at a large medical supply company, has been working on a time-sensitive document and IMs keep popping up and misdirecting his attention. *Who are they from?* Caryn, Julian's Gen Y employee. *What is the message?* Did Julian get the e-mail she sent him 30 minutes ago asking how he liked the report she completed? *What's the urgency?* Caryn's been waiting 30 minutes wondering why Julian is taking so long to respond when it only takes a second to find out the capital of Madagascar.

When will they stop? They won't, because this is the new generation of communication: texting, Webinars, instant messaging, social networking, and online meetings. The ship has sailed for classic business practices. Communication has become about speed and demand for immediate return. The way we have always expected in-person communication to be an interaction where one person says something and the other responds, we now expect the same speed of communication to occur in electronic form, whether the person is sitting across the office or across the world. It has created a global impatience, especially among Generation Y employees, who have been communicating with the latest and greatest advances in communication technology because their family PDAs were keeping track of Mommy and Me Yoga, play dates, and every other type of activity under the sun.

In addition to the global impatience, we have been witnessing a slow decline of formally written language as tech speak increases. Gen Y is so used to writing/texting/typing in short hand inspired by social networking sites, texting, and e-mails that their ability to communicate in written, formal format has rapidly deteriorated (for example, beloved pronouns such as "you" have now been replaced with the ever reputable "u"). The preference for digital media communication has also contributed to a rapid decline in basic verbal communication, because the informality has spilled over into day-to-day in-person interactions.

Digital media communication has also contributed to the creation of various "online" personas through social media Websites such as MySpace, allowing people to take on a public personality that is often quite different than how they present themselves off line. These multiple personas, coupled with the decline in appropriate verbal and written communication and interaction, has had a direct impact in the workplace with regard to emotional intelligence, reputation building/destruction, and basic workplace etiquette.

Due to the rapid technological advances and the resulting positives and negatives associated with them, a large generational gap in communication has occurred. This has caused the creation of various generational dialects and a clash between generational cultures. (For example, "What!?" instead of "Excuse me, I didn't hear what you just said.") Because the style and culture of communication is different in each generation, what often results are situations steeped in miscommunications, misunderstandings, and conflicted thoughts and feelings.

Did this really happen? Yes!

A text message was sent from Erin, a Gen Y employee, to David, her Gen X coworker, asking for his input on the next steps of a project. David received the text and tried to call her. No answer. However, within five seconds David received another text message from Erin stating the following: "I'm only texting today, not talking on the phone." David texted back: "Well, I'm only talking on the phone, not texting." That was the end of that conversation and no input was given or taken for the project to advance.

Back to the (psychological) basics

Mom and Dad taught me my first words, but technology taught me how to speak

Generation Y was born during a time of some of the most rapid technological advances affecting how they communicate with regard to speed, the type and quality of language, and without consideration of time or location. These rapid technological developments and the subsequent transformation of communication have competed with parents' ability to teach, influence, and develop language skills (speaking and writing words correctly and politely). In the past, we learned language and communication style from our parents, our teachers, and our friends. Nowadays, communication may begin with parents, but develops and transforms based on technological exposure. Once a child develops the basic foundation of language and communication, both verbal and physical, other influences start impacting quality and preferences. However, preferences also exist based on different personalities and generational groups.

Technology influences on communication by generation

Veterans:	*Rotary telephones, in-person conversations and meetings.*
Boomers:	*Touch tone telephones, use of memos.*
Generation X:	*Cell phones, phone conferences, e-mail.*
Generation Y:	*Smart phones, Web-based social networking, Webcams, text messages, instant messaging, and so on.*

As Generation Y grew up, technology exploded and a whole new language developed. Marc Prensky, an internationally acclaimed speaker, writer, consultant, and designer in the critical areas of education and learning, makes the distinction between digital natives (Generation Y) and digital immigrants (all previous generations). Digital natives have always had technology as a huge part of their world and digital immigrants have had to learn how to incorporate new technology into their lives. As with any of us who learn a second or third language and retain our native accent, Prensky comments on how digital immigrants retain their "accents/foot into the past," where technology is not second nature. Prensky gives the following examples of how we can observe digital immigrant accents: printing out a document to edit it rather than editing it on the computer screen or asking someone to come into your office to see an interesting Website rather than e-mailing them the URL.

Being a digital native also goes hand-in-hand with global connection. More specifically, the world of technology has enabled us to stay in contact with just about anyone, anywhere, and at anytime. We can also meet people we did not know previously if we contact them and they are willing to communicate back, such as an instant pen pal. Having access to massive social networks has always been a way of life for Generation Y. Individuals from more seasoned generations who sign onto those social networking sites for the first time are having fun playing catch up with old friends from grade school and college, whereas, Generation Y has always communicated within their social networks in this manner. There are phenomenal opportunities to network with the use of technology, and Generation Y has friends and friends of friends that they stay connected with, even if only virtually. Their contacts can be called upon whenever needed for business or for personal matters.

Communication is communication—it doesn't matter the medium, only the message

As Gen Y has entered the workforce they have changed interpersonal and business communication more so than any generation before. They brought their new language with them, often confusing other generations and contributing to the decline of appropriate workplace language and the formality of communication. This is evident today with the advent of texting, IMing, and Gchat as a common and imperative piece of business transactions. Who would have thought you could have five different conversations at once via IM versus one via the ancient telephone?

Most Boomers would agree that part of successful communication at work includes calling your clients on the phone, meeting people through face-to-face networking, and communicating verbal respect for your superiors. It could be argued that Generation Y may conflict with other generations in this way because they feel that communication is communication regardless of the medium used. More specifically, Gen Y's are just as comfortable being assigned a project or communicating with their bosses via text, e-mail, or IM as they are being assigned a project or communicating with their bosses during a face-to-face meeting. Either way, they get the message. Similar to any "language" the native speakers or first-generation speakers of any "new" language will assign and develop rules, structure, grammar, and even "ethics" to communication. It is different, but not necessarily lesser. Y's refusal to communicate other than electronically and briefly is because they do believe it is really okay and just as effective.

Which generation are you?

Boomer says: Let's schedule a meeting in my office at noon.

X says: This is getting too complex, let's stop IMing and talk on the phone.

Y says: Text me, IM me, but please don't call me.

On one hand, this preference allows for rapid communication, which theoretically can positively influence performance time. On the other hand, the preference to communicate via digital media instead of more traditional forms of communication has resulted in missed opportunities to develop and refine basic communication skills, such as understanding underlying verbal cues of communication (for example, tone or voice), nonverbal cues (for example, facial expression and body language), and real life (versus virtual) relationship building opportunities. Gen Y's preference for rapid communication often results in miscommunication and misunderstanding negatively impacting performance in general. Further, for many members of Gen Y it is difficult for them to leave their electronics idle while engaged in work that does not require, or in some cases permit, them to be near any electronic communication devices.

Did this really happen? Yes!

"As oncology nurses at a children's center we rarely have time to use our cell phones or jump on the computer for e-mail, so I leave my cell phone turned off during the work day. If any emergencies come up everyone knows I can be reached through the center's landline. Imagine my shock and disgust when I walked into one of our treatment rooms and found two of our brand new nursing student interns laying on the sterile treatment beds texting on their phones."

Max C., oncology nurse,
Children's Outpatient Clinic

Communication technology has changed the way we all "speak" to each other

Generation Y has never been without computers, e-mail, or cell phones. They have spent very little time, if any, communicating via handwritten or typed letters. They are unaware of life prior to texting or instant messaging. They are unaware of what it was like to have something to tell someone and have to wait to call them until they get home to their telephone. Google and Wikipedia replaced encyclopedias and actually "looking something up." Facebook and Internet dating has replaced the blind date or the setup (or when they happen they are usually via social networking sites or e-mail introductions). Basically, Gen Y has never had to delay gratification, which has been reflected in the tech speak formalized by this generation.

If you are not a member of Generation Y you will probably need a handy guide to help you understand what most acronyms typed via text message and instant message really mean. Communicating via digital mediums has changed communication, resulting in the creation of an Internet language, as seen here:

What Is Gen Y really saying?

Match the following commonly used acronyms:

1. 2G2B4G	a. *Never mind. I have to go.*
2. BTW JM w u	b. *See you later. I am going to sleep.*
3. NVM G2G	c. *Nothing much, you?*
4. Gr8t CUtnite	d. *By the way, I was just messing with you.*
5. CYL-zzz	e. *Great. See you tonight.*
6. nmu	f. *To good to be forgotten*

answers: 1-f; 2-d; 3-a; 4-e; 5-b; 6-c

When primarily communicating via technology short hand, it becomes a challenge when asked to write a document via regular old long hand. Many who have become accustomed to tech speak have had the experience of writing out a formal e-mail and accidently putting "u" in place of "you," "btw" instead of "by the way," and "ru" instead of "are you." Along with the creation of Internet or tech speak, tech inflection has also developed with non-verbal replacements, such as the infamous LOL (laugh out loud) or smiley-face emoticons.

This verbal and non verbal communication replacement has paved the way for a generation that has trouble corresponding when it comes to more traditional forms of workplace communication such as face-to-face interaction and written documents. For example, some managers we spoke with complained that, even with spell check, Gen Y is known for handing in documents with spelling errors on a frequent basis.

A leader says:

"I am at a loss for what to do when grown adults hand in documents that have improper spelling and grammar mistakes. This situation has increased since Generation Y has become a part of the workplace. I always hand the poorly written documents back and ask them to proofread and fix it before they hand it in again. The reaction I get baffles me. I get comments such as, 'Come-on' or 'Are you kidding me?,' or 'You get what I'm trying to say here,' and my favorite, 'It's an electronic copy, just press spell check.'

Erica Lui, consultant,
PR & Marketing Firm

Over-reliance on spellcheck or auto correct does not necessarily help with word selection (that is, then vs. than) or proper grammar. In addition, informal verbal communication and the non-preferred communication methods at inappropriate times seem to be on the top of the list of frustrations for managers and supervisors when it comes to this generation. Further, another frustration includes Gen Y's difficulty understanding when it is important not to multitask (one ear bud in, texting or constant checking of phone, improper eye contact, or not looking "attentive" at work).

A leader says:

"There has been quite a change in public modesty and decorum with this generation. I've noticed that this generation just tends to say what they are going to say, even if it's inappropriate. If you challenge them on it, you'll hear a shocked and confused Gen Y say, 'What, what did I say that was wrong?'"

Stevie Ray, executive director,
Stevie Ray's Improv Company

Because Gen Y's are at the beginning of their careers, they are often in "trench" positions (for example, positions with direct contact with customers, such as sales and customer service), which are the positions representing the company on a daily basis. On one hand their social aptitude has proven to be wonderful in these positions, especially because they say it like it is, are open to getting along with everyone, and have wonderful, creative ideas about how to streamline technology and non-technology related work tasks. However, their preference for digital media communication and the resulting problems with regard to written and verbal skills, as well as basic communication skills, has created serious problems for companies working with this generation, as well as developing this generation as contributors and eventual leaders. One of the areas that has been most impacted by the preference for digital communication is in the area of Emotional Intelligence (EQ), which is a key factor in being a successful leader.

The decline of emotional intelligence

We build relationships by communicating with others, no matter what type of interaction. Although we are born with innate emotional intelligence potential, our upbringing, surroundings, and experiences influence its development. Although the term *emotional intelligence* (EQ) is relatively new in business culture, it is a concept that psychologists have worked on developing in clients since the beginning of our profession. After all, enhanced EQ translates into better relationships and enhanced self-awareness, goals that are common in the therapeutic experience. See the following box for a brief tune up on the concept of emotional intelligence:

Shrinkwrapped

What is Emotional Intelligence (EQ)? EQ has been an important concept in the writings of psychologists Howard Gardner, Peter Salovey, and John Mayer. Daniel Goleman has studied, written, and expanded the concept of EQ into a popular and important personal development concept. He believes that there are four domains of EQ, and the more developed, the higher EQ someone has.

› *Self-awareness—Knowing and understanding what you are experiencing.*

› *Self-management—Managing and expressing your emotions in socially appropriate ways.*

› *Social awareness—Recognizing and having empathy for how others are feeling.*

› *Relationship management—Inspiring and influencing others, conflict management.*

Emotionally intelligent leaders are individuals that energize others through their enthusiasm, inspiration, ability to truly reflect on situations, skill of empathizing with others, and ability to manage themselves in emotionally and socially appropriate ways. Leaders who are high in EQ are extremely effective in understanding what their supervisees need in order to learn, develop, and grow. Overall, EQ is important in leadership and the development of leadership qualities. These qualities develop through experiences and insight gained through positive (and negative) social interaction, and personal exploration contributing to enhanced self-awareness.

We argue that technology has contributed to an ailment that has the potential to stunt the growth of emotional intelligence. The fact that we text people instead of calling them, e-mail people instead of having in-person meetings, play video games instead of kickball, and say happy birthday via Facebook or Friendster rather than visiting a friend with a birthday cake says a lot about our culture and how the importance of relationships or what defines relationships has changed. Also, in the "old days" of communication, when there was a problem, you dealt with it, face to face, which helped one develop skills in conflict resolution, problem-solving, and perspective taking, all factors that contribute to emotional intelligence. Having a preference for digital communication allows one to "log off" if things get too difficult, often stunting consequences for behaviors that serve as teachable moments and opportunities to enhance one's emotional intelligence.

As stated previously, positive and negative social interactions coupled with our upbringing, environmental surroundings, and experiences transforms and influences whether our emotional intelligence will shift from potential into action. The more we play video games instead of interacting with each other, or send e-mails instead of getting up from our desks to talk to one another, the less likely we are to hone qualities that are inherent in excellent leadership: understanding and applying the basic fundamentals of social awareness, being emotionally aware and in tune, and adaptive self-awareness and self-management skills to name a few. This is especially true of our digital natives, our next generation of leaders. They have only known a life infused with tech speak and bring that way of speaking into the workplace.

Technological exhibitionism

Coupled with the decline in EQ in the workplace due to communication changes comes what we call technological exhibitionism. Due to the fact that this generation has been raised on communication mediums that allow for public exposure on a constant basis, there seems to be little shame in allowing the entire world to know what you are engaged in at any particular moment, whether it be good or bad, on digital platforms such as Twitter, MySpace, Facebook, Friendster, FriendFeed, YouTube, written or video blogging, and so on. When the Internet serves as a mask of anonymity, you can create any persona you would like and present that "person" to the rest of the world. This is quite alluring to children and adults alike, hence the constant news headlines of Internet bullying and Internet blunders.

Because this generation has always been engaged in technological exhibitionism, it carries them to the workplace, which causes a whole new set of HR issues. More specifically, individuals in hiring positions have told us that they often learn a lot of information about potential employees by doing a three-minute Google search before their potential employee arrives for their interview.

Did this really happen? Yes!

"When I interview potential new employees, I do research on the Internet about them prior to meeting them. One time a guy applied for a position with us. I researched him before I scheduled the interview and found his MySpace profile, which had this crazy, antisocial stuff on it. I contacted him and told him that I had come across his MySpace profile and encouraged him to present himself differently in the public world, because the Internet is how the public world and any potential employer can dig up information about you. I thought I was giving him good advice. However, he responded back via e-mail and said, 'Whatever, forget you, forget you.' All I could think was, 'Were you really serious about working for me?' I'm a potential employer trying to give you the heads up about how you are harming your reputation and your employability."

Angelo Anastasio, CEO,
Greenable

In addition to pre-hiring problems, managers and HR personnel alike often run into problems with younger employees who use Internet-based resources, such as blogs, as their sounding board for work-related issues or relationship issues, often impacting the reputation of the company, and, ultimately, the reputation of the employee. These issues tie into aspects of self-management, which is a key component of emotional intelligence. Because we live in a voyeuristic society when it comes to the Internet, serious hiring, retention, and engagement issues are developing because of the tendency toward technological exhibitionism among this generation.

How it plays out: three advantages of Gen Y's communication style

"Communicate unto the other person that which you would want him to communicate unto you if your positions were reversed."

—Aaron Goldman

PDAs as babies + digital media options = creative ways to increase the bottom line

This is the generation of instant communication and information. As a result, Ys see no limitation in communicating with anyone, anywhere, and anytime. With boundless communication opportunities, infinite possibilities exist to correspond in creative ways. Because of this, Generation Y has contributed to unbelievable advances in communication technology. Take for example 24-year-old Mark Zuckerberg, founder of the social networking site Facebook. This Harvard dropout has completely changed the face of communication as we know it by connecting people via a technology platform that is relatively simple and clean. It has reconnected people, rekindled old flames, and launched businesses and social connections globally. He is a visionary. He is also a member of Gen Y that was raised on a whole new idea of what communication is (that is, a way of connecting that no longer conforms to traditional mediums and has no boundaries).

If we created workplaces that allowed Gen Y to excel using their native language, imagine the creative possibilities that Gen Y employees could invent for companies. Their development of language and communication has been shaped by their exposure to technology. It is part of their identity and values. They are not stunted or afraid of new advances. They are completely open and excited about what is possible. This means that less energy is wasted on being confused and apprehensive, and more energy is spent on being creative and imaginative with regard to different ways to exchange ideas and information. Ultimately, letting your Gen Y's go forward with their natural intuition and connection with technology will create new and creative possibilities for your company. Let your Gen Y's create and utilize their means of communication and do what they do best. Do not fear their love of technology; instead use it to your advantage.

A leader says:

"Some of the Gen Y employees I hire are better than me at everything because they've been doing it since they were born, where as I had to go to school and learn it. They are constantly connected, so they are up to date on every new change. I guess it's the same with every generation. I was that person to my parents who wondered how I was able to move Pacman so fast across the screen. But this generation is just on top of everything technological and it's pretty amazing what they can do and how they can help with their ideas."

Angelo Anastasio, CEO,

Greenable

Communication multitasking as a way of life

Gen Y has been over-stimulated from the beginning. In fact, it can be easily observed that there is a strong discomfort for many in this generation when they feel under stimulated and unconnected. They are used to several forms of media going at the same time. Information is entering the minds of Gen Y's at lightning speed and they are taking it all in just fine, often consolidating a days worth of information into hours. Gen Y is used to multiprocessing and multitasking, and they are more effective with this than any other generation. They are more comfortable with receiving and sending multiple forms of input and output of information simultaneously.

Although research has consistently shown that multitasking is not effective because one's quality of thought deteriorates through time when attending to multiple tasks, perhaps there is an evolutionary change occurring among Gen Y's, because they have always been exposed to multiple forms of media simultaneously. Although limits may have to be put in place, recognize that Gen Y employees can often produce quality work with music in their ears and IM messages all over their screens.

A leader says:

"Liz is one of our star employees at our small family run agency. She starts out most of her days by sitting down at her cubicle, surfing the net while instant messaging with at least three friends, blogs about her previous night, has her iPod playing her favorite songs, and texts a friend to discuss lunch plans, all while working within a document that she has been preparing for the meeting scheduled later that day. Liz is effective at doing all of these activities at the same time. It works for her. It's the only way she has known. I'm her boss and used to complain about Liz and her other Gen Y cohorts, and then I

> *came to the realization that this is simply the way this Generation communicates and works. They are multitaskers and they are good at it. I just wish I could get a little more eye contact and more frequent social graces from time to time."*
>
> *Kathy, founder/president,*
> *Family-owned wine business*

The benefit of massive networks

Unlike any other generation before, Gen Y has had the ability to develop relationships instantaneously regardless of location. Traditional forms of communication, such as letter writing, has invoked a derogatory name (snail mail) and the idea of pen pals is an outdated, foreign concept. Access to people anywhere at any time, because they have always had access to global communication, has created a generation that has enormous networks to call upon for anything from social networking to idea development to the enhancement of business relationships. This can be an incredible asset to companies as it allows for input from a global perspective, inclusive of location, age, gender, and industry. Gen Y's various communication mediums and levels of connections with others has created incredible opportunities for businesses. However, the people that supervise and work with Gen Y need to think outside of the box and recognize the power inherent in their massive networks.

A Gen Y says:

Bruce, a Gen Y marketing assistant related the following story to us: "My boss put me in charge of a fundraising event for the company. This event was going to bring a lot of publicity to our company, so I needed to get as many people as possible to come to the event or donate money or items. I have a lot of friends locally, but that wasn't going to cut it. I basically put out a request on a few of my networking sites, and it was amazing how that worked. I basically exceeded my boss's expectations and really surpassed what we expected the event to draw in. It was really cool too, because I even had some donations sent to me from overseas from people who were friends of my friends."

Three challenges of Generation Y's communication style

"You can have brilliant ideas, but if you can't get them across, your ideas won't get you anywhere."

—Lee Iacocca (1924–)

I need it now, I need it now, I need it now, I NEED IT NOW!!!!!!!

Because Gen Y has had information at their fingertips faster than a speeding bullet at all times, their expectations regarding pace of information transfer appears to be slightly higher than the average Boomer employee or even Gen X employee. Gen Ys often get frustrated and impatient with the pace of typical communication and information exchange in most corporations today. These expectations need to be managed as the workplace environment shifts to incorporate the pace of technology, and thus quicker and more effective communication.

This generation, who has always been able to search and find the answer for anything, repeatedly asks "why" when told to do something, even when the "why" is inappropriate and the behavior is just expected. Although some of this may be an age-related issue, most Boomers and Xers did not question their bosses requests and demands as much as Gen Y tends to do. This is not necessarily a reflection of disrespect or insubordination, it is more of a reflection of the need that this generation has for knowing that their work is important and meaningful.

A leader says:

"Their worlds have become so much easier, so they are spoiled with regard to their expectations in general and with regard to speed. Most companies are generally slow with their processes and tend to be slow reactors. Generation Y gets frustrated by this and then the question of 'Why?' starts coming. After all, they have an answer to everything in an instant with their username and password."

Angelo Anastasio, CEO,
Greenables

The obituary of face-to-face contact

With Facebook, Friendster, Google, MySpace, texting, and all the other phenomenal communication creations, social grace and etiquette has shifted. Books and blogs talk about Internetiquette (digital media etiquette) rather than the etiquette of face-to-face communication. Body language, eye contact, and the importance of tone when communicating feeling has been exchanged for acronyms (for example, great vs. gr8t), capital letters (are we still meeting today vs. MEETING TODAY?), and choppy conversations with no clear ending (because there are rarely goodbyes in the world of texting; instead you simply stop responding). Overall, by communicating via digital media, one misses out on the opportunity to hone basic communication skills, such as understanding underlying verbal cues to communication (tone of voice), non-verbal cues (facial expression and body language), and real life (as opposed to virtual) relationship-building opportunities.

In addition, digital media has created an entirely new set of mixed messages and miscommunications. For example, when someone appropriately says, "I love you" during a phone conversation, most likely, if you love the person, you will return the verbal gesture. However, when someone texts you a question or a statement that has normally been a verbal gesture, and you do not bother texting back because it takes too long, a misunderstanding or miscommunication is bound to occur. What about those stories we have all heard about an e-mail ending up in the wrong person's inbox? Also, as stated before, the social networking movement inspired and furthered by this generation has created technological exhibitionism where individuals can create personas online that are different from how they present themselves offline. These different personas can have a huge impact on reputation in an organization or for an organization, because the Internet is basically a free-for-all voyeuristic playground.

HR chimes in:

"You need to encourage a culture of etiquette within your organization as it shifts from traditional communication to digital communication. For instance, talk to your Gen Y employee about not sending inappropriate e-mails at work no matter what may happen to them if they don't immediately forward the e-mail to 100 people."

Helen, HR executive,

Marketing research company

Language barriers: goodbye, adios, adieu, TTYL

With the new language of technology and communication style that Gen Y has brought into the workplace, a metamorphosis of interpersonal and business communication has occurred. This transition has left other generations confused, because they were not raised with the same style of tech speak communication. Language formality (grammar, spelling, and face-to-face talk) is no longer a necessity for this generation. This has caused a language barrier, because most people tend to be impatient and easily frustrated when miscommunication occurs. Also, when different generations have different values regarding communication (for example, Boomers feel it is important to talk to superiors in a formal manner), messages can be mixed and can seem disrespectful. Consequently, this can create issues with regard to promotions, increased responsibility, and even the desire to work within intergenerational teams.

Gen Y is often observed to be more impatient than other generations. Perhaps they are actually just more advanced and comfortable with their language/use of technology, which is inherently quick. Because they are the experts in technology and their expectations within technology tend to be high, Gen Y may come off as impatient (which they are), annoying (which they can be), whiney (which is understandable given their perceived frustrations), and ultimately these characteristics can impact their reputations, work relationships, and ability to succeed.

Did this really happen? Yes!

A physician who owns a small group practice received an e-mail from one of his Gen Y assistants that read, "Yo Scott, I know you denied my request for a day off next Friday, but I really need to take off and you'll need to reconsider cause I can't come in that day."

Dr. Scott Michaels, owner and director,
Medical Group Practice

The takeaways so far...

If you remember nothing else, take away the following:

> Like it or not, the way we communicate has changed.
> Digital media communication is a native language to Gen Y while the rest of us are learning a second technological language.

> The style and culture of communication is different from generation to generation, which often results in miscommunications, misunderstandings and conflicted thoughts and feelings.
> Technological communication advances can potentially hinder the development of emotional intelligence.

You can use Gen Y's communication style to your advantage by:

> Realizing and appreciating their native technological communication skills to create new possibilities for your company.
> Understanding their effectiveness at communicating within multiple mediums simultaneously.
> Noticing the possibilities to add global perspectives, as well as a wide variety of social connections, via technological communication.

Watch out for Gen Y's tendency to:

> Show impatience with the time it takes others to respond to them.
> Have a preference for digital communication over face-to-face communication.
> Communicate in ways that produce mixed messages due to their culture of informality within digital communication.

Now it's time to take some action. Here are the coaching solutions that we recommend to enhance the positives and manage the negatives of Generation Y's communication preferences.

Coaching solutions: building on strengths and addressing the challenges

Gen Y's communication style and technology fluency has created several opportunities within the workplace to harness their strengths for the benefit of the organization and to help them develop their own leadership skills. At the same time, these wonderful qualities have created unique challenges that will require strategic coaching to help minimize the potential problems these characteristics may have on organizational functioning and their own leadership development.

No-brainer coaching solutions

CS1: The green memo

The larger the company the more difficult it is to make sure all of your employees are getting the latest information about changes in policies and workplace happenings. Most of us, even if by the slim chance we like reading memos, usually read them and discard them, often forgetting the message within minutes. Gen Y has been known to disregard information that is conveyed on paper. So why not take their lead and start creating "green" memos or information in the form of daily or weekly blogs, podcasts, or message boards? In order to utilize their technological talents, creativity, and their tendency to be socially conscious put the blog/podcast responsibility on one of your Gen Y employees. In fact, you may end up going from a simple blog or podcast to a dynamic, engaging, digital communication platform that allows for interaction and/or various enhancements.

Why it works

In light of the global environmental issues facing our world, it is important for organizations to consider alternatives to traditional forms of communication, and this is one of those alternatives that have been embraced by most mid-sized to large companies. Not only is it a fast, easy way to communicate company information, it can also make a positive impact on the environment, and send the message to all employees that your organization is conscientious and up with the times. Paper is out, digital is in. The good news is that you are saving trees, and saving company dollars along the way. Not only will this benefit your company, it will give your Gen Y employee the new and exciting responsibilities they crave, offer them a platform for recognition, and tap into their talents.

Important note: Using an internal company blog can be useful for memos that are in need of a response, (such as company attendance, policy changes, signing up for projects, and so on). However, difficulties can arise when people begin using the company blog for their own personal commentary on how they feel about the company policy or project. We recommend that you have rules that are clearly defined and boldly displayed about this communication approach, so there is no question. Also, assign one of your employees, preferably a Gen Yer, to serve as the monitor of these blogs, so that problematic responses are brought to the attention of the appropriate manager to be worked through. Remember, this is an opportunity to teach Internet etiquette, ultimately shaping the culture of your organization.

CS2: *Staying young by exercising your communication muscle*

If you have resistance about communicating in new ways, just remember how your grandparents or parents may have refused to learn new technology and how they sadly just "got old," not understanding how to work something that came so easily to you. Maybe you even tried to teach them and they just found it easier to have you do it for them. Or maybe they were good students and excited to learn the new technology.

Be excited to learn the new and flex your mental muscles. An effective way to "stay young" is to at least have a general understanding of the latest and greatest in technology. There are so many digital forms of communication with new models popping up all the time. In fact, by the time this book is published it is quite possible that there will be a whole new technology fad that has "changed our world forever." Forget trying to keep up—focus on how to get started instead by asking the knowledgeable Gen Y employee sitting right next to you. Not only will this allow your Gen Y employee to enhance their training skills and patience, it will engage them and communicate a message of respect and value. It is likely that taking this time to learn, understand, and begin using the latest in digital communication will save you more time in the future and you will be included in the loop of information you were missing. Further, you may engage your Gen Y employee and work on relationship-building along the way.

Why it works

First of all, flexing your mental muscle by engaging in any kind of learning, especially learning that challenges your comfort zone, keeps you younger. Brain research has shown that when we learn novel concepts and new strategies to problems we develop our brains (by creating new neuronal connections and pathways). Not only are there personal benefits, there are benefits to the workplace. More specifically, when you step outside of your comfort zone and also begin using alternative forms of communications, you may find that messages can be transferred in a more efficient way, ultimately enhancing performance and productivity. Try and remember that once you learn how to do something, it often becomes second nature.

Important note: Although we are recommending taking the plunge and embracing new forms of digital media communication, we are not recommending that you stop stressing the importance of face to face contact with your Gen Y employee. Just as you may prefer face-to-face contact, they prefer digital forms of communication. Stepping outside of your comfort zone and encouraging others to embrace different forms of communication is an imperative part of grooming successful leaders.

Idea into action

A mid-sized advertising company started to realize that there were extreme differences in communication styles between their Gen Y employees and other generations. Although the Gen Y employees did not spend as much time in each other's offices, they tended to know more about each other in every area of their lives. They seemed to be more cohesive as a group. One of the more seasoned employees grabbed a few of his Gen Y coworkers and spent time learning new ways to network and communicate digitally. He reported that while he still struggles a little bit, he is excited to be able to send a quick instant message question to a coworker who can respond instantly. This employee also stated he was happy to learn how to set "away from desk" or "do not disturb" messages on the IM function on his computer.

CS3: Gain free consultants worldwide at the touch of a few buttons

Ever have a problem that needs to be solved and wish you could speak to someone who had the answer? Well, your Gen Y employee may have the answer you need or, more likely, they probably will know how to find it for you. Gen Y's are sharing their stories, questions, and continual connectedness with "friends" (virtual and real life) worldwide. When a need arises, do not be shy to ask your Gen Y's if they have any contacts that would be helpful.

Why it works

This coaching solution works because Gen Y has always been connected to others via social networking sites. Although it is second nature for them, it is not for the rest of us. Learning from Gen Y how to increase our global social networks will not only benefit our personal lives, but it also has the potential to benefit productivity when it comes to business. You never know who you will meet, or how they can help.

CS4: Allow them to multitask because they are going to do it anyway

One of the individuals we interviewed, Justin Foster, founder and partner of Tricycle, a brand development company, brought to our attention a very interesting and controversial approach he uses with his Gen Y clients. He indicated that when he runs his branding meetings, he gives a speech at the beginning of the presentation stating that everyone should feel free to "text, IM, or whatever" during the presentation, but just turn off their ringers and avoid taking cell phone calls while he is talking/presenting. Justin explained to us that trying to prevent this multitasking from happening just creates subversive behavior, because they are going to do it anyway. He reminded us that this generation is fabulous at multitasking, and that they are more capable of taking in different forms of communication at the same time. To make them do what they are already going to do in a subversive manner takes more energy away from their ability to focus in the first place, so you might as well let them go with it. Although this may be a controversial recommendation, it may be worth giving it a try.

Important note: Although many Gen Y's are great at multitasking, if you find that productivity is diminishing in the workplace among your Gen Y employees (or any employee) due to multitasking, then put limits in place.

Why it works

Generation Y are effective multitaskers. It is difficult for the rest of us to comprehend how they are able to be productive with their attention focused in several directions, when the rest of us may have trouble, from time to time, focusing in on one area. When you allow them to work in the ways that they have worked their entire lives, it takes the stress away from having to monitor them, and lets them be responsible for themselves and their own information gathering.

Brainer coaching solutions

CS5: Earning respect through the "I" instead of "You"

If someone was unhappy with something that you did and said would you be able to hear the message and change accordingly, or would you get self-protective? Would you agree that it would be more beneficial if this person that is unhappy with you said, "I feel this way based on..., what are your thoughts..., what can we do about it? This not only focuses on the subjective feeling of the person expressing him- or herself, but offers a possible solution. Speaking in "You did this..." statements often leads others to feel attacked and focus on defending themselves, as opposed to listening and seeking solutions. Remember for the majority of your Gen Y employees they are used to people being happy to hear what they have to say. They are used to hearing positive feedback for their unique ideas, and they are used to treating those older than themselves as equals. Pull the blame away from them, and stick it in the middle of the two of you to find possible solutions.

Here are some examples:

> When you walk by my office and say "yo" like I'm your friend, or tell me about your weekend adventures of drinking and being hung over you are being disrespectful and not treating me the way I deserve to be treated as your boss.

vs.

> I really value our working relationship and want to develop it further but want to tell you that it makes me feel uncomfortable and disrespected when…

> When you show up to work wearing your nose ring, it really reflects badly on you and on our team.

vs.

> I really want you to succeed in your role here and would like to talk to you about how I can help you present yourself in a way that will help you get the respect you deserve in this company. I've noticed that the people in our company who wear their nose piercings automatically are dismissed by the higher ups. Although that may be unfair, I want you to be heard without pre-judgment.

> You aren't listening to what I am saying

vs.

> I felt unheard during our meeting today.

Why it works

In our day-to-day relationships, we complain that one person may make us feel angry, sad, or hurt. The truth is no one can make you feel any way. Our feelings are based on our own interpretations of a situation. So, when we say to someone in our personal lives, "you are making me so angry," that is actually not correct. We are feeling "so angry" because of the way we interpreted a situation. The same goes for the workplace. This recommendation forces you to take ownership of the emotion you are experiencing and allows for communication of emotions to be received without defensiveness. It is an important concept and one that is reflective of maturity, good communication, and good leadership. This recommendation works because it steers clear from blame and instead focuses on the message being heard.

CS6: Set the limits

Although organizations put rules and regulations in place with ease, sometimes there are difficulties with the follow through. With the decline of written and verbal communication along with the rise of technology exhibitionism; workplace etiquette, self-control, and self-awareness need to be taught and modeled. This is especially true because many of your Gen Y employees are currently in "trench" positions, representing your company on a daily basis either on the phone, in person, or virtually. Here are the limits we suggest putting in place:

1. Don't accept documents that are not adequately proofread or do not meet your expectations.

2. Stand your ground when a Gen Y refuses to communicate with you or your colleagues in a format that is appropriate.

3. Do regular searches on the Internet to prevent technology exhibitionism that can tarnish the company name or the employee's reputation.

We know that it is hard to manage your frustration when a Gen Y employee refuses to turn in spell-checked documents or refuses to pick up the phone when you call and instead texts you back. Therefore, the root of this solution is not about standing your ground or setting your limits, it is about *how* you stand your ground and *how* you set your limits. More specifically, depending on how you approach setting these limits, you can either have a teachable moment that strengthens leadership skills and fosters emotional intelligence, or you can have an absolute disaster that results in an insulted Gen Y employee who thinks you are completely unreasonable.

Your Gen Y employees are used to a certain way of communicating and a certain level of exhibitionism on the Internet. You cannot simply say, "STOP." You need to offer an explanation and model good leadership. This is received best using coaching solution 5 (earning respect through the "I" instead of "You") along with a real conversation about the importance and role of reputation building for leadership development. Building one's reputation is not something that young people first think about when entering the workplace. It is often after several errors and reputation killers that one starts to understand the importance of developing professionalism, reputation, and respect. Because this generation is probably less equipped than others to develop professionalism in the current Boomer created culture, it is imperative that Gen Y supervisors take the time to advise and coach them about reputation building and professionalism in a non-abrasive, empathetic, and professional way. A productive conversation with your Gen Yer about how you would like to see them excel (and that sometimes their choices may get in the way of that) models for them good leadership and helps them understand that you are invested in their success.

Important note: Some of your Gen Y employees may look at their current job as "just a job" without much interest in promotion or development of their skills. It is important to weed out your Gen Y employees that you feel have growth and leadership potential from those that are floating through your company as a stepping-stone. Focus your energies on those employees who want the guidance and feedback (or whom you feel will shine with this guidance). As with all development, change only happens when the party involved desires it.

Why it works

This generation does not like being told what to do or how to do it. Simply saying "stop" is not going to work. This generation requires and demands an explanation for just about everything they are asked to do. Approaching problems in a calm and productive way and focusing on helping them build their reputations will have more impact than simply admonishing their behavior.

CS7: The Gen Y expert

When there is a problem in a company, experts are recruited to offer recommendations, possibilities, and solutions. So why not engage your internal technology experts? Because new technology is coming out every day and companies are constantly rolling out new technological solutions, often with the intent of making work life easier (yes, we know, it never seems to get easier), we suggest developing your Gen Y's mentoring skills by placing them in charge of mentoring individuals who struggle with technological changes as their "go-to" person and educator. When you are rolling out new technology let them lead the teams for training if it is a subject in which they are already proficient.

Why it works

Not only does this provide for team and relationship building, it creates an opportunity for your Gen Y employees to develop needed leadership and mentoring skills such as patience, enhanced verbal communication skills, emotional intelligence, and training/education abilities. In addition, placing your Gen Y in this role can increase feelings of value, worth, and acknowledgment. These feelings can bolster a healthy and well-earned dose of confidence and self-esteem.

Idea into action

A large insurance company would frequently go through adaptations and changes in their technology platforms. These changes, often created and implemented because of the belief that they would make work easier, not only made the processes more difficult, but created incredible amounts of frustration among staff being forced to learn the new technology. To counteract this problem, management decided to recruit Gen Y volunteers to engage in the creation, implementation, and rollout of all new technology projects. The company found that having feedback from people that were adept at technology "user" ability helped the staff create better technology platforms. In addition, giving their Gen Y staff opportunities to hone in on their education and training abilities truly enhanced their overall communication skills.

Big-brainer coaching solutions

CS8: Building social relationships through communication the emotionally intelligent way

Gen Y is not interested in "being controlled" or hearing commands about how they should behave, how they should look, how they should think, and how they should feel. They crave authenticity and self-expression with what they wear, how they speak, relationships that they build, and how they work. When they believe that their authenticity and self-expression are thwarted, there is bound to be a consequence reflected in their communication, performance, and mutual respect with intergenerational colleagues and/or bosses.

We build relationships through the way we communicate with others. Emotionally intelligent leaders can help Gen Y's learn by example how to develop relationships, build trust and respect, and eventually mentor others. Because this large generation has a profound impact on the culture of corporations, it is imperative that the bosses who supervise Gen Y do so with the goal of helping them to function productively and effectively by helping them effectively communicate (no matter the medium); thereby, improving workplace relationships.

We have thoughts and emotions, and we use written or spoken words and nonverbal gestures to get our message across. Understanding our emotions and being able to recognize the emotions of others is essential to be able to communicate effectively and demonstrate emotional intelligence. No matter the medium you are communicating through, understanding how you are feeling about an incident or situation is important to developing and practicing emotional awareness. Try the Pause-Reflect-Choose (PRC) technique developed by Daniel Feldman and remember to take a few deep breaths.

The PRC Method by Daniel Feldman:

1. *Pause before reacting to a situation.*
2. *Reflect on what is causing the emotions or reactions being experienced.*
3. *Choose the appropriate reactions that will make the situation turn out well.*

Be conscious of this process as you supervise your Gen Y employees. Remember you are not only leading them in the short run, you are developing them to lead and contribute successfully in the future.

Why it works

The more we understand ourselves (our thoughts, emotions, and actions) the stronger the relationships we can build and the more effective we are at leading others. It is easy to be reactive to situations as they occur and just simply respond without reflection. However, taking a moment to "pause, reflect, and choose" will increase your emotional intelligence in the area of communication resulting in enhanced relationship management.

Coaching solutions simplified

Coaching Solution 1

Title: The green memo.

Purpose: To put your Gen Y employee(s) in charge of relaying important information in an environmentally friendly, cost effective way.

Outcome: Promotion of good organizational "green" ethics and incorporation of the strengths of your Gen Y employees' computer expertise.

Coaching Solution 2

Title: Staying young by exercising your communication muscle.

Purpose: To help other generations step outside of their comfort zone with regard to technology and communication.

Outcome: Performance and productivity improvement, intergenerational relationship building, and expanded technological awareness.

Coaching Solution 3

Title: Gain free consultants worldwide at the touch of a few buttons.

Purpose: To enhance idea creation and information gathering via a larger, global network.

Outcome: Tap into your Gen Ys natural talents, a broader pool of ideas for solutions.

Coaching Solution 4

Title: Allow them to multitask because they are going to do it anyway.

Purpose: To allow your Gen Y employees to multitask and prevent your own burn out from trying to get in the way of their natural inclinations to multitask.

Outcome: Prevention of managerial burn out, time saver.

Coaching Solution 5

Title: Earning respect through the I instead of you.

Purpose: To model good communication form in the workplace.

Outcome: Improved leadership skills, communication skills, and emotional intelligence.

Coaching Solution 6

Title: Set the limits.

Purpose: To model appropriate communication for your Gen Y employees and teach the importance of reputation building and professionalism.

Outcome: Enhanced professionalism and interception of potential reputation damaging behaviors.

Coaching Solution 7

Title: The Gen Y expert.

Purpose: To use your Gen Y employee's innate talents with regard to technology and to give them initiatives to lead or be part of that will in turn develop their leadership and mentoring skills.

Outcome: Enhanced education and training skills, increased organizational commitment, recognition for Gen Y, and improved mentoring skills.

Coaching Solution 8

Title: Building social relationships through emotionally intelligent communication.

Purpose: To enhance communication skills and improve relationship management skills.

Outcome: Improved leadership skills, enhanced emotional intelligence.

——Chapter 6——

I'm the Boss of Me: Work Ethic and Generation Y

"By working faithfully eight hours a day, you may get to be a boss and work twelve hours a day."

—Robert Frost

> *While writing this book in our local hipster Gen Y coffee shop we asked 24-year old Faith, who was recently hired at a large local corporation, to answer the question, "How do you like your new job?" Part of her response was as follows:*
>
> *"Honestly? Don't make me come in from 9 to 5 dressed in my parents' uniforms of suits and pantyhose. Flexibility, creativity, talent, performance-driven, casual, and hip are the buzzwords of my generation; not stiff, obedient, rigid, and structured. What's wrong with you people? We are electronically connected at all times, don't worry. I'll get your phone call, I have an iPhone, and I'll get the e-mail or document you need to give me, I have a MacBook! Why do I have to work in a cubicle during the hours you set when I can work better and more efficiently on my own time, on my own couch, with my cool dog Sam right by my side?"*

Generation Y's work ethic is quite different from the philosophy that most businesses have been built upon (formality and structure). Traditional business practices of a 9-to-5 work day (or many more hours), business formal attire, staying in companies for your entire working tenure (until retirement or they lay you off), in-person meetings and "work before play" philosophies are rapidly being interrogated under the bright lights of this generation's will. Quite frankly, the size of this generation is demanding that the workplace conform to their ethic of work. A clear tug of war between the old and the new is ensuing, and the new is beginning to win out. This generation is forcing organizations to take their needs seriously and to figure out creative ways to recruit, retain, and engage them. They are demanding dissolution of the old rules, forcing companies to consider the integration of work and life, flexibility, and a redefinition of what work looks like and how it is done. They want to be acknowledged for what they have to offer, and at the same time, they want to be respected for the fullness of their lives and their philosophy that work is part of life, not their lives.

Back to the (psychological) basics

What do dependability, reliability, dedication, conscientiousness, adaptability, loyalty, pursuit of accomplishment and achievement, motivation, responsibility, accountability, and hard-working all have in common? They are characteristics that are evident in someone who demonstrates a strong work ethic. Perhaps some chuckles or a loud "Ha!" erupting from your mouth as you read the characteristics that make up a strong work ethic and think about how they apply to your Gen Y employees. Perhaps you agree with the floating theory that Gen Y is lazy and does not have a good work ethic. We think this is untrue. They just have a *different* work ethic and prefer to work on their own terms, which is what earns them their reputation of being frustrating, lazy, and unqualified. The truth is, Gen Y may demonstrate all of the qualities associated with a strong work ethic, but because work is integrated into their life rather than a reflection of their life, certain characteristics (dependability, accountability, and loyalty) may be strong in their relationships and nonwork related commitments while other characteristics (hard-working, pursuit of accomplishment, and achievement) may be reflected more during the traditional work hours.

Work ethic needs to be judged relative to a generation and a culture not relative to the way another generation was raised. Work ethic is developed from the upbringing, lifestyle, and the cultural pulse of a generation. Where Boomers were raised to work within the confines that the corporation dictated, and respond and change to the needs of the organization, Gen Y's were raised to speak their minds, challenge the confines that the corporation dictates, and have expectations of their employers to change based on their needs. These philosophies are clearly different and clearly influenced by the differences in the child-rearing philosophies and schooling philosophies established in each generation.

The clash between the two work philosophies is so visible these days. Boomers and Veterans, who have been in leadership positions for the past several decades, have shaped the corporate landscape and the subsequent expectations of what work ethic should be in companies today. However, Gen Y, the fastest growing segment of the workforce who will outnumber Gen X by 2010, is demanding that the corporate landscape change to reflect and mesh with their relationship to work and their values. The basic unspoken rules that have governed corporations for the past 100 years or so are being intensely challenged.

Traditional Work Ethic	**Gen Y Work Ethic**
Work comes first.	*Life comes first.*
Distinction between work and personal time.	*No distinction between work and personal time = work/life integration.*
Follow the rules no matter what.	*Follow rules that work and make their own rules if they do not.*
The boss deserves respect.	*Equality and respect is given only when earned.*
Senority = promotion.	*Talent = promotion.*
9 to 5 with overtime expected.	*No defined work clock.*
Work is based on hours.	*Once work is finished I can leave for the day, even if it's before 5 p.m.*
Preference for face-to-face contact.	*Preference for digital contact.*
Dress the part at all times.	*Dress the part when necessary.*
Will change to meet the needs of the organization.	*Expect the organization to change to meet their needs.*

As the leaders who developed and/or furthered the traditional rules that governed corporations for the past century prepare to leave the workforce and the future leaders begin to take over, tension is becoming more intense and the "traditional" opponents are beginning to succumb to the pressure. Frustrations are mounting from both sides as supervisors and managers are losing good Gen Y employees because they "have a life to live," "like showing off their tattoos and piercings," and "don't want to work these hours." It is funny to note, however, that the same people who raised their children to demand and expect everything are the same leaders complaining that their figurative children are demanding and expecting everything. Let's take a look at how this happened.

Mixed messages

Every generation develops their idea of what work is based on the reactions and experiences of those who raised them. Gen Y was raised by the Boomers and older Gen Xers who felt that getting a "good job," working hard, and saving your money was a priority. They were also the same people who got laid off, lost their pensions, had the highest (first and second marriage) divorce rates, and became the poster children of the term *mid-life crisis*. So on one hand, their children, Gen Y, learned that working hard, long hours and saving your money leads to getting laid off or not being able to retire because of the stock market crash of 2008 or the loss of all of your hard-earned money when your company filed for bankruptcy. They also learned that if you work hard and save your money, you get to ruin your relationships, have a complete meltdown in your prime, and get a plethora of stress related illnesses and problems such as heart disease. So to sum up the formula that Gen Y witnessed: work hard + work long + be obedient + save your money = get screwed.

At the same time while this message was being inadvertently delivered, the Ys were raised to be right no matter what and speak their minds no matter what. They were protected from fault, mistakes, and blame at all costs. The combination of being right no matter what, parents teaming up with their child against their teachers, everyone winning at everything, and being able to move back home with your helicopter parent at any age, influences one's ability to be adaptable, motivated, dedicated, responsible, and accountable, especially once entering the workplace. When Supermom or Superdad flies in to protect you when you mess up, it becomes difficult to muster up enough motivation to accept responsibility for your behaviors and to hold yourself accountable for finding a solution to a problem.

As a result, this generation was raised to be a little spoiled, a little coddled, and a little perfect in the eyes of the beholder (and a little annoying in the eyes of everyone else). The unintentional consequence of being coddled and protected was leaving out the inherent lessons that come with pain, mistakes, and fault. Ultimately, the biggest mistake was giving their Gen Y children the organic, non-farm raised, high-antioxidant, low-mercury fish from the farmer's market, but forgetting to teach them how to fish in the first place. With this lesson comes the best qualities of the Boomer work ethic; perseverance, staying power, and a healthy balance of acceptance and expression of change—qualities that are now often lacking in the Gen Y ethic of work.

Did this really happen? Yes!

"One of my Gen Y employees brought me a receipt for a taxi for $33. The city is 7 square miles, so I asked her why the taxi cost so much. She said, 'I had to stop to pick up shoes for the event.' I ended up paying for the taxi because sometimes it's easier to throw money at the problem than to rationalize with them, because in their eyes they did nothing wrong."

Claudia Ross, owner,

Cross Marketing

Three advantages of generation Y's work ethic

"Work is either fun or drudgery. It depends on your attitude. I like fun."
—Colleen C. Barrett (1944–), president emeritus of Southwest Airlines

Enough with work-life balance already…it's time for work-life integration

For years, work-life balance has been the "it" thing. Wellness programs, consultant recommendations, and company initiatives have all pushed the importance of this concept, which stresses that balance is the only way to keep workers satisfied. In the midst of the work-life balance movement, Americans are working harder, being paid less, and suffering from more work-related medical and mental health problems than ever before. Is this really America's idea of balance? Balance implies a desirable point between two competing or opposing states. However, when did work and life become competing interests or take positions on opposite ends of the spectrum? This is where Gen Y can teach us all a little lesson. Generation Y has demanded that the concept of work-life balance be replaced with the concept of work-life integration. Gen Y does not see work and personal time as separate entities. Rather, they see work as something that should be integrated into their lives rather than all encompassing. This generation is the first generation to refuse incorporating the term *workaholic* into their vocabulary.

This philosophy can be viewed with resistance, or welcomed as a breath of fresh air. It forces us, even if through frustration, to look at ourselves, look at our priorities, and hopefully relax a bit more. Gen Y has shown us that the work still gets done when it is integrated into life, rather than when it is forced into the confines of a 9 to 5 work day that supposedly creates "balance." This is probably one of the most powerful and influential philosophies that Gen Y brings to the table and something that other generations might want to consider embracing. Perhaps if more of us adopted this philosophy, the zombie-like culture of the overworked, stressed out, and irritable would benefit.

A leader says:

"I have this Gen Y entrepreneur with whom I consult. She absolutely blows me away. She is a photographer and she asked me to give her marketing advice to grow her photography company. She works really hard, by anyone's standards, and has this amazing entrepreneurial spirit and mind. She rides her bike to work so she can squeeze in her exercise while contributing to the environment. She does lots of trading of services to expand her network base and get the word out. She does get stressed out like the rest of us, but she laughs about it—she is incredibly light-hearted. In fact, she just put on this huge breast cancer fundraiser targeting brides called 'Get Hitched, Give Hope' and pulled all these sponsors and partners together to enhance her business network and help people meet each other, while raising money for a cause that she believes in. She is all about integrating what is important in her life and the mission of how she wants to run her company. And she's not even 30 years old!"

Whitney Keyes, owner,
Whitney Keyes Productions, LLC

Let me work the way I know how to

When Generation Y employees are able to work their own way, not only do they excel, but also they tend to think outside of the box of traditional solutions. Their developmental exposure to, and use of, digital media outlets provides them with more resistance to classic corporate groupthink (that is, poor decision-making that discourages creativity and individual responsibility). This generation is demanding changes in the culture of the corporate environment. Perhaps these demands seem outrageous, but let's take a closer look at what the demands are, and what they would actually mean.

Flexible work days and work weeks:	*Happier and more productive Gen Y's.*
Less stringent requirements on dress:	*Happier and more productive Gen Y's.*
Less formality:	*Happier and more productive Gen Y's.*
Improved work relationships:	*Happier and more productive Gen Y's.*
Increased access to digital media:	*Happier and more productive Gen Y's.*

Truthfully, wouldn't we all be happier if things were a little less uptight and work got finished just as effectively? In addition to happier Gen Ys, these demands really do have a positive impact on the corporate culture. When people feel like their jobs are flexible and incorporated into their lives, rather than running their lives, they work more effectively. Access to digital media outlets often allows for easier communication and enhances work flexibility. If managed correctly they can add new-found time to people's schedules (unless the individual has become cracked out with their digital media addictions). Less formality in the workplace, when possible, enhances comfort and ease of communication, which can ultimately have a positive impact on workplace relationships, as long as everyone is comfortable with the less stringent formality, and as long as it is not misused. Overall, many of the expectations that Gen Y has could actually be very beneficial for all generations, and for corporations, as long as they are integrated in a useful and effective way.

I got game...trust me

Gen Y has some serious initiative. They have been told that they will do great things and have been given opportunities to excel. When they enter the workforce they are often ready to hit the ground running, as long as they are not stifled by micromanagement and receive their acknowledgment and rewards along the way. Kevin Mercuri, president of Propheta Communications, states, "This generation is young and hungry and all of their lives they have been told they are great and will succeed and they realize that they have been living their entire life up to this point to succeed." Kevin also notes that the pressure to do great work not only is inherent, but this generation recognizes early on in the work experience that great work gets noticed. Since getting noticed is important and motivating to this generation, everything that they do must be great, and subsequently they have difficulty with the job duties of their entry level positions. Trying to do great work is often coupled with disappointment in their current positions and leads to burn out, boredom, expectation of different responsibilities, desires for quick promotions, and loyalty issues. However, the pressure to succeed and to produce great work often goes hand-in-hand with amazing initiatives.

A leader says:

"The last company I worked for was having problems and was basically in a death spiral. Despite the company's downward spiral, this guy who was 23 years old at the time was a fan of our company because of the games we produced and stopped by our booth during an industry fair expressing his interest in working for us. He was on his way to getting his MBA and asked if we would be interested in having him do some work for us. I was honest with him and told him about the company's situation, but he still jumped at the opportunity. By the time he finished up school and got to us about a year later, the company was really going downhill, but he still came aboard. By the time he left, only a few years later, I was handing him whole departments to manage because I was completely amazed at what he could do. He would nail it and move on and nail the next one. It was that 80/20 rule. He handled 80 percent of what was important. By the time he was done working for us he was doing community management, international distribution, started a new program and revamped our Website. On top of handling all this other stuff, he was taking on initiatives that didn't come from me. He worked at his own pace, his own hours, and did his own thing. Although his approach wasn't always typical, he completely amazed me in his ability to accomplish almost everything, as long as he was left to do it his own way without my interference."

Scott Dodson, COO,

Divide By Zero Games, Inc.

Three challenges of Generation Y's work ethic

"Son, if you really want something in this life, you have to work for it. Now quiet! They're about to announce the lottery numbers."

—Homer J. Simpson, *The Simpsons*

> *"Our Gen Y staff has been a challenge because they all want flexibility to come and go at their discretion. Prior to us putting in an attendance policy (which was a new phenomenon for us with this generation), almost everyone was late to work and did not seem to care. They got here when they got here. Since putting in the attendance policy, performance has greatly improved. While implementing the policy we heard constant complaints that we were harassing them and the policy was unfair. We also have continual challenges with everyone wanting to work from home, even though they were not sick and can function enough to come to work. They want to work from home because they don't want to use their sick time benefit. We have recently developed a Work at Home Program (telecommute) and only allow those who qualify (high performers, no disciplinary actions, good attendance) to participate. As a call center we have regular schedules and a seniority policy to change a schedule. Many Gen Y applicants will not work for us because they want more flexibility with schedules than we can offer."*
> *Mary Hobbes, VP of human resources,*
> *Large pharmaceutical company*

It's not my fault

Although this generation has initiative they frequently lack accountability, because for most of their lives they have been shielded from fault, blame, and mistakes. When they receive constructive criticism, they are often the first to blame their boss, their coworkers, or their "bad day" rather than accepting responsibility for their mistake or inadequate performance. This lack of accountability is often coupled with a lack of perseverance and qualities that are related to good work ethic. The frustration that ensues among managers often outweighs the positives that stem from their initiative and desire to do great work, not entry-level work. This is a developmental issue that can be addressed with good planning and coaching, as addressed in our coaching solutions section.

A leader says:

"I see a lot of initiative with this generation, but not a lot of accountability. They get an A for enthusiasm, but when it comes to being accountable for their actions—executing and following through—where are they?"
Emily Scherberth, owner and chief connections officer,
Symphony PR & Marketing

Gen Y's work clock and work expectations

We know that for this generation spending time with friends and family and engaging in meaningful life activities and social causes is much more important than doing the daily 9 to 5 grind. Although this generation has it right when it comes to integrating work and life, and incorporating more flexibility into the workplace, sometimes (okay, a lot of times) they take it too far and at the expense of their work responsibilities. Managers and HR personnel are often taken aback by requests for special accommodations regarding what hours are worked and where work is performed (at home versus the office). For example, the following story reflects the Gen Y work clock:

Did this really happen? Yes!

"We were opening up a new retail store. Upper management was at the new location and they were in constant contact with us back in the home office. It was a really big day and we all had a tremendous amount of work to do. One of my Gen Y employees said to me, 'Oh, just wanted to let you know that I'll be leaving at 4:30 today because I have a nail appointment.' I was completely astonished by her outlandish request during one of our busiest days and responded, 'No you don't, cancel it.'
J. Joyce, marketing director,
Large retail chain

Gen Y employees often expect that accommodations and special exceptions will be made to immediately address their concerns. There is an underlying assumption that Gen Y expects organizations to change to meet their needs instead of adjusting to meet the needs of the organization.

Did this really happen? Yes!

"One of my Gen Y employees hired for data entry was visibly upset so I asked her what was wrong. She began crying and stated, 'I was working on a computer all day at school today and can't possibly look at it anymore today.' I thought, 'But I hired you and need you for data entry—if you can't do that job today then I don't need you to work here.' She expected me to change her job to meet her needs, rather than meeting the needs of the company, which would require her to work on the task she was hired for."

Stevie Ray, executive director,

Stevie Ray's Improv Company

Lifelong loyalty?

Lifelong loyalty to a company is a concept that was inherent to the Veteran Generation and passed down to the Boomer generation. However, Generation Y children watched their loyal parents get laid off as the economy shifted in the 90s. The resulting message was that company loyalty was a value developed by people, but not honored by corporations. This message has been heard loud and clear by Gen Y, resulting in major retention and engagement issues. It is not uncommon to hire a Gen Y employee, spend significant dollars training them, and then lose them because they are unhappy with the workplace culture. It is estimated that it can cost three to six times a person's salary to hire them, train them, and provide them with the resources they need to get up to speed to be productive. This generation is costing corporations excessive dollars a year because loyalty is dead. It must be noted, however, that although corporate loyalty is dead, loyalty to friends, bosses, and colleagues is stronger than ever. This is one of the few generations that works more for the boss then for the company. This means that nurturing your relationship with your Gen Y employee is imperative.

The takeaways so far...

If you remember nothing else, take away the following:

> Be careful when comparing the work ethic of the Boomers to the Y's; they are different and both offer wonderful opportunities for growth and development.

> Work/life integration, flexibility, the ability to be heard and recognized, and being challenged with exciting work responsibilities are important to this generation.

You can use Gen Y's work ethic to your advantage by:

- Embracing work/life integration.
- Providing for working conditions that play to their strengths rather than working against them.
- Providing them with opportunities that will give them a chance to show their initiative.

Watch out for the tendency for Gen Y to:

› Have trouble hearing they may be incorrect and the tendency to avoid taking accountability.

› Expect that companies will adjust to meet their needs rather than adjust themselves to meet the needs of the company.

› Be loyal to their friends, coworkers, and managers, not the company.

Now it's time to take some action. Here are the coaching solutions that we recommend to enhance the positives and manage the negatives related to this generation's work ethic.

Coaching solutions (CS): building on strengths and addressing the challenge

As Gen Y entered the work force, their coworkers and supervisors began seeing the rise of a whole new philosophy of work. This has only grown louder and stronger as Generation Y's numbers within companies have grown. Their different way of thinking about how they would like to work and ideas of what work should be has created significant challenges and opportunities for the workplace.

No-brainer coaching solutions

CS1: As with any healthy relationship pick your battles

Gen Y has always been given free range of speech, dress, and attitude. They are used to being fully accepted for however they think, dress, communicate. If some behaviors are inappropriate in the workplace then of course they should be addressed. However, it is important to ask yourself if what you are seeing is a real workplace concern or a matter of difference in personal preference? If it is a workplace problem, attend to it. However, if it is a personal preference that will have no impact on productivity or the end result, such as the way someone chooses to communicate (for example, digital or in-person), then pick the battles that are worth fighting.

Why it works

We believe this is more of a managerial or leadership philosophy than a coaching solution. Although Gen Y employees are young enough to be shaped and groomed into successful contributors and leaders, there are certain values that are ingrained that will be very difficult to change. Just like in a relationship or in therapy, you cannot change someone's core values and ethics, you can only encourage good choices, inspire the motivation to grow and learn, and help strengthen the qualities that make a person outstanding. Hence, choose your battles wisely and do not waste time on the issues that truly do not impact productivity or the end result.

Idea into action

Scott Dodson, COO of Divide By Zero Games, Inc., is an example of a leader who has learned this value, and has effectively incorporated it into his leadership style. The gaming company he works for was founded by a Gen Y individual and has a significant number of Gen Y employees. He describes the work culture as being very flexible—people wear what they want to wear, and there really is not much barrier to communication. In fact, one of the Gen Y leaders at the company often wears a kilt to work, commando style. Scott chooses to take a laissez faire approach to his leadership, which allows his Gen Y people to thrive. He stated that he will intervene if choices or behaviors get in the way of getting the job done.

CS2: The holistic approach

As we discussed, Gen Y is all about work/life integration. Because this is the case, the traditional 9-to-5, work hard to get promoted, formality of corporations is not going to cut it with this generation. There's no room for stuffiness. In order to engage this generation and enhance their loyalty to your organization (remember, it costs a significant amount of money to recruit, train, and then lose an employee), you must begin to accept that they might have a different approach to work and life than you do. Get to know your Gen Y employees, find out what they do outside of work and allowing them access to Myspace, Facebook, Twitter, and LinkedIn (in moderation). Honoring their styles will help them honor yours. Remember, this is the generation that feels it is important, and rightfully so, to earn and grow respect based on understanding and relationships, as opposed to getting respect just because you are the boss. Integrating opportunities for people to get to know one another (via a company Intranet, company-wide or team get-togethers) are not only good for your Gen Y employees, it is good for everyone. Remember, this is an area where Gen Y has it right. If everyone understood the importance of work/life integration (versus balancing everything on a tight rope) there would be far less emotional and physical problems ailing our society.

Why it works

This coaching solution is something that is very simple, but effective. When you try and understand the people you work with, it makes them feel like you are invested in knowing them and building a relationship. Understanding Gen Y's preferred way of work not only helps them work better and more effectively, it demonstrates care and concern for their well-being.

Idea into action

We spoke with one Gen X executive, Justin Foster, founder and partner of Tricycle, who operates a branding company with his Gen Y business partner. He talked to us about how they had to get used to each other. Justin indicated that his partner has always needed to "work on his own terms." The whole idea of showing up for work at 8 a.m. and leaving at 5 p.m. is foreign to his Gen Y business partner. He describes that "workaholic" is not even in his lingo. He works when he works, but always completes the task well and on time. As his business partner, Justin has had to put aside the business traditions he is used to and get used to the change in order to make the partnership work. His Gen Y business partner has also learned how to adjust, and recognizes that in order to run a business you have to respect how other people work. Therefore, this flexible give and take with traditional methods has worked wonders for them.

Brainer coaching solutions

CS3: The incubator

Gen Y employees, when given the right opportunities to create and function within their own work ethic, can be incredible rainmakers and idea makers for your company. In the spirit of this characteristic, we present to you the coaching solution of "The Incubator." We already know that Gen Y is taking their time to "figure it out" and appreciates space and range to work without being told what to do. Because this is their style, we recommend implementing a program that allows your employees to work collaboratively with others to develop innovative company solutions that may be out of their direct area of work. A committee can be formed that reviews all initiatives to see if they are feasible or useful to the company. If the committee approves an idea or initiative provided by an employee, a team can be formed of interested individuals (even if the project falls outside of their area of expertise or job description) to develop the proposed idea. Develop this as an optional job description. Having this as an optional part of people's work experience allows them to think outside of the box, as well as work on projects that may be outside of their typical day-to-day jobs.

Why it works

This solution works because it takes people outside of their typical daily grind and gives them an opportunity to be creative as well as beneficial to the company. When people operate outside of their area of expertise, they often bring a fresh approach to an idea. Allowing people to be innovative in areas of interest, rather than areas that they may be used to working on, gives them the opportunity to develop their skills and interests.

Important note: Make time for this innovative and creative process to occur. Of course set boundaries of how much time can be spent, but try not to treat it as any less important. This is a strategy that engages people, shows value for their talents, and builds and/or strengthens loyalty.

Idea into action

One example of this kind of program is occurring at a company called I Love Rewards. Founder and CEO, Razor Suleman, states that he has designed Vision Committees, which come up with different ideas and projects. If an employee is interested, they can spend 20 percent of their time working on a project of interest outside of their regular job description. He told us about one employee, Zak, who was one of the company's lead software developers. Zak wanted to work on getting PR for the company, so he pitched the PR Vision Committee idea to Razor. It was chosen, so he recruited a team made up of people from various departments and together they set initiatives and goals for the committee. Each member was able to spend 20 percent of his or her time per week, working on the PR Vision Committee. They had a lot of success and from there the company decided to create a Marketing/PR department.

CS4: Leadership development classes (aka business etiquette classes)

Gen Y operates under a different set of rules and standards in the workplace. These often do not meld with the current business culture, causing unnecessary problems and generational clashes. With this generation, the corporate culture will change. However, we have heard from several Boomers who have concern over the importance of leaving a legacy by directing and grooming Y's to be as successful as the next generation of leaders. How can this be undertaken with such a demanding, outspoken generation? Teach them business etiquette under the guise of leadership development courses. Everyone wants leadership development and everyone benefits from this type of training. Traditional leadership development courses include discussions around emotional intelligence, vision, values, integrity, communication, influence, and image. We recommend that you tie into these concepts the basic traits and qualities, such as business etiquette, that you want to see develop among your future leaders. These kinds of courses will not only be highly valued by this generation who thrive off of continued education and training, but will also benefit them by helping them learn the ropes. It is important that they feel like they are still expressing who they are, while also integrating some of the proven qualities that make a leader great. A few bells and whistles never hurt anyone. Your leadership development courses can include the following topics:

Title	Added Benefit
How to be influential	Address the issue of chain of command.
Professional appearance	Address clothing and piercing choices.
Effective communication	Address the issue of respect and talking appropriately to your superiors and customers.
Rising to the top	Address the rules and policies of the organization including issues related to flexibility and work clock.
Emotional intelligence	Address the issues of taking and giving feedback.

Why it works

This generation thrives on mentoring, training, and continuing education opportunities. A training related to developing their leadership skills can also provide a setting where those who are trying to groom them to be effective can help them understand the importance of basic etiquette in a non-demeaning way. For example, it is much easier to talk about the importance of professional image and the role it plays in the business environment than it is to ask someone to remove their eyebrow piercing when presenting the company product to a firm that targets age 65 or older.

Big-brainer coaching solutions

CS5: *The integrated development plan*

Corporations spend exorbitant amounts of money on coaching and development services for their upper management every year. However, many lower-level positions are neglected in that respect, even though several of those employees will eventually fill upper management positions. We recommend putting time, effort, and some dollars into the personal development plans of your Gen Y employees, especially the ones who have great potential. Think about it for a second: If the first organization that you worked for out of college was wonderful, would you have stayed if they noticed your talent and invested in you from the very beginning by helping you accomplish your organizational and personal goals? Of course! This is at the core of talent management and retention.

We are calling this an integrated development plan, rather than a work development plan, because it should honor the importance of work/life integration. Quality time should be spent on this task and it should be revisited (at the minimum bi-annually) to ensure that the individual is carrying through with his or her own development, and that the company is following through with its commitment to the employee. In addition, expectations and timelines should be attached to each area that is explored in this development plan. This personal development plan should include the following facets:

1. Career development within the organization.
    a. Defining the career trajectory that makes sense for the individual.
    b. Defining the type of work and projects of interest.
    c. Defining the skills and talents necessary for this trajectory.
    d. Defining the learning and training opportunities to support the progress of this career path.

2. Educational and learning opportunities.
   a. Establishing important educational and learning benchmarks that should be accomplished to integrate business and personal goals.
   b. Incorporation of benchmarks or milestones for appropriate mentoring and coaching opportunities.
3. Personal opportunities.
   a. Outlining personal goals (travel, family).
   b. Defining how the corporation can support these life goals.
      i. Flexible work schedule.
      ii. Flexible work environment (for example, telecommuting).
   c. Defining personal life values.
      i. Financial well-being.
      ii. Emotional well-being.
      iii. Physical well-being.

Why it works

The reason why this coaching solution works is very simple: it shows significant interest in your Gen Y employee. Taking the time to actually help your Gen Y employee envision their personal and professional goals tells them that you are invested in their growth and development. In addition, following through with this task and expecting follow through from your Gen Y employee enhances their accountability, responsibility, and perseverance, which are all important qualities of a strong work ethic.

Important note: If you drop the ball with this coaching solution, it will be noticed. If you are going to commit to doing the integrated development plan with your employees, it must be incorporated, revisited, and referred to throughout the employee's career with your organization.

CS6: Rotations

Because several Boomers demonstrated lifelong loyalty only to be laid off, they encouraged their children, the Y's, to take their time exploring opportunities and not settle down with any one job (or romantic relationship for that matter). Because Gen Y children are taking their time with career decisions, rather than fight it, go with it (particularly since this is one of the qualities that leads to excessive job hopping, which we all know is incredibly expensive for corporations).

How do you join in on allowing your Gen Y time with their career decisions? If possible, offer rotations (full time or a percentage of the time) in the workplace, similar to what medical schools offers their students, so they can get a wide range of experiences and figure out where their interests lie. For example, if someone in finance is interested in marketing then 10 to 20 percent of their time may be spent working in the marketing department. Obviously, not every company can afford to take this approach; however, offering this solution satisfies your Gen Y's inherent desire to operate outside of the box and to try new things while encouraging company engagement. Companies can do this to help their employees find their best fit and develop a wide range of skills. An added benefit to this solution is that when employees understand the operations of different departments, they tend to perform better because they have a more comprehensive knowledge of how all the parts of the system work. If you are unable to offer this solution because of company needs, allow a certain percentage of their time to be spent on a project or solution for another department, as suggested in this chapter's Coaching Solution 3, "The Incubator."

Important note: If you are able to implement this, make sure that you allow your Generation Y employee to stay with their rotation long enough so that they develop a deep understanding of how a department works, again contributing to operational success. It is probably best to base the rotations on projects, so that there is a clear beginning, middle, and end.

Why it works

This solution lends itself to Gen Y's natural developmental process of wanting to take their time to "figure it out." It allows for exploration and enhancement of different skills and talents. Not only does it benefit the employee, it benefits the organization because it helps leaders see where their Gen Y's are most skilled. It also brings fresh ideas to a department with different people rotating in and out. In addition, it helps people realize what one is not good at. Rotating can build fortitude through working on a project in an area that is not a strength, and empathy and respect for workers who do those jobs all the time. This solution also benefits the company by building more well-rounded employees who do more for the same pay.

Coaching solutions simplified

Coaching Solution 1

Title: As with any healthy relationship pick your battles.

Purpose: To decide which Gen Y behaviors are important to manage and which to accept.

Outcome: Managerial stress reduction, increased workplace satisfaction for all.

Coaching Solution 2

Title: The holistic approach.

Purpose: To allow Gen Ys to operate within their comfort zone and their preferred mode of work.

Outcome: Improved work relationships, workplace comfort and enjoyment.

Coaching Solution 3

Title: The incubator.

Purpose: To allow your Gen Y employee to tackle different projects outside of their area of expertise, while allowing for cross training and new, fresh perspectives.

Outcome: Cross-training, reduced boredom, fresh perspectives, employee retention.

Coaching Solution 4

Title: Leadership development classes (aka business etiquette classes).

Purpose: To teach necessary business etiquette while providing leadership development training and education.

Outcome: Enhanced leadership skills and professional interpersonal skills, education about current expected business behaviors.

Coaching Solution 5

Title: The integrated development plan.

Purpose: To invest in the development of your Gen Y employee by helping them to map out their personal and professional path within the organization.

Outcome: Talent management, enhanced retention and engagement.

Coaching Solution 6

Title: Rotations

Purpose: To allow your Gen Y employees to learn different departments and get involved with different activities for a specified period of time.

Outcome: Enhanced loyalty, strength/talent identification, and skill-building.

──Chapter 7──

I'm Qualified for the Position, but I'm also a Specialist in Socializing: Generation Y and Relationships

"Interdependence is and ought to be as much the ideal of man as self-sufficiency. Man is a social being."

—Mahatma Gandhi (1869–1948)

> *"I own a PR firm and most of my Gen Y employees feel that the events we throw serve a dual purpose: work and a dating service. They see these events as a time to be social when I see it as my job and their job. One example of this was when my company was overseeing a PR event for a band. One of my Gen Y employees, who loved the band, approached one of the musicians at the event. After the event, she asked for a few days off to go visit her family in Chicago. I looked at the band's Website and, low and behold, the band was touring Chicago during the same time period she was visiting her family in Chicago. A few weeks later, I received an e-mail from her saying that she had to leave for Europe the next day with her parents and that she would be gone for two weeks. The e-mail was very dramatic claiming that her parents would be very upset with her if she didn't get the time off. Needless to say, I looked up the band's tour dates and not surprisingly, the band was doing a two-week tour in Europe at the same time as her 'family vacation.' I sent her an e-mail back telling her to have an amazing time and that I considered her e-mail a resignation and that this would be her last day. She was completely shocked and did not understand why she was being let go and responded that she was being 'forced' by her parents to*

> *go to Europe. I never called her out on it, but of course she and her musician boyfriend had pictures of their European tour posted all over Facebook. They think I'm stupid and don't know how to check up on their lies. She had a wonderful gig with me. I just don't understand when times changed so much that someone would be willing to give up such a great job for their social life."*
> *Claudia Ross, owner,*
> *Cross Marketing*

Most would agree that having friends both in and out of work and keeping connected with people is an important part of all of our lives. However, as a whole, Generation Y has prioritized their relationships over work and other commitments. They are a generation more comfortable in activities that involve socialization. Advancements in technology allow anyone to be reached anywhere within a few seconds. This has helped forge a generation where the lines between work time and socializing time are blurred.

Socializing and relationships are so much of a priority that if you ask a Gen Y individual what is important to them about work, relationships with co-workers will most likely be at the top of their list. Ask a Gen Y why they chose to work for a particular company and you just may hear, "because my friend works there." Due to the level of importance and priority placed on relationships, it is often also seen as a challenge as they begin their new careers. Results from SelectMinds.com's 2006 survey of 2,002 individuals between the ages of 20 and 29, suggest that, "When transitioning into a new job, Generation Y ranked 'cementing relationships with colleagues and supervisors' (41 percent) as their number one challenge, ahead of learning the new job responsibilities (27 percent) and adapting to a new company culture (33 percent)." Because relationships and socializing are such a priority for this generation, it has become a challenge for companies in their retention and engagement strategies. Not only do businesses have to make the work attractive and interesting to engage this generation, but they also have to foster a workplace culture that supports relationship building and connection in order to retain them.

Did this really happen? Yes!

J. Joyce, a Marketing Director at a large retail chain, relayed the following story to us: "I walked by Rachel's office, one of my Gen Y employees, a few weeks ago and noticed someone I didn't recognize sitting at her desk with her feet up reading a newspaper. An hour later I walked by again and the person was still there, in the same position, still reading the newspaper.

> *I found Rachel and asked her who was in her office and she said to me,*
> *"Oh, that's my friend Desiree. I think you met her at that customer party we*
> *had a few weeks ago. She just came in to hang out with me at work today."*

Back to the (psychological) basics

The shift in how we socialize and stay connected with others

"It's just business, it's not personal." For Generation Y it is all personal, and then there is business. It is the relationship that may recruit that fabulous Gen Y to your company and will definitely have an impact on their happiness at work more so than it has for any preceding generation. For other generations, relationships are very important; however, work often takes precedence. How many times have you said to one of your friends, "Sorry, I haven't called you back, I've been busy at work," or "I'd love to meet you after work but it's been a long day"? As previously mentioned, Generation Y does not hold a distinction between work time, and personal time and if pushed to choose, a majority of Generation Y employees would say that relationships with others is the priority over work responsibilities. This is evident in the importance that Generation Y places on their work relationships, and the importance of constant contact with their friends outside of the office during work hours. Additionally, Generation Y places more emphasis on their relationship with their boss than any other generation. They have been known to leave companies if their boss has decided to leave.

Gen Y is used to maintaining friendships through digital mediums. This is not to say that getting together with friends, face-to-face, is not important. However, digital communication via e-mails, texts, and social networking sites holds a similar value. Due to the fact that "e-socializing" is acceptable, Generation Y experiences a different ease of friendship maintenance than other generations. Sending quick text messages, updating the status section of their Facebook profile, or Tweeting thoughts and comments is a form of instant friendship maintenance. This ease of friendship maintenance and the demand for work/life integration translates into constant friend communication throughout the workday, whether tolerated by the company or not. It is so second nature to communicate constantly with friends that reminders to use work time for work are often ignored.

> **A Gen Y says:**
>
> *Bruce, a Gen Y marketing assistant states, "We're used to doing things together. I've gotten my friends jobs from places that I've worked and they have done the same for me. You spend so much time working, why not work with your friends and become friends with those you work with every day?"*

Overall, this generation establishes, expresses, and maintains their relationships with others in such a drastically different way than any generation before. Due to the acceptance of e-socialization, they are the first generation that has been able to maintain strong, long-term friendships, regardless of time, distance, or location, from the beginning of the friendship formation. In addition, because they were always involved in activities that emphasized social building and social time (for example, play dates as infants, kid-oriented classes before they could talk, daycare, preschool, and so on), they often can talk about several close friends that they have had since they were born. Even if they lost contact with some of those friends they made when they were three years old, they have had opportunities to re-connect through social networking sites such as MySpace and Facebook. Connecting with others through social networking sites is second nature, and just as acceptable to this generation as face-to-face friendship maintenance, and they are teaching the rest of us to start to reconnect through these mediums.

Born and bred to work in teams

Being able to work on a team is an important quality required in companies today. For all generations, except for Generation Y, teamwork is an unnatural phenomenon to which employees have been forced to conform, engage in, and learn to master. For many it is most natural to work independently and be self-reliant. However, for Generation Y, working on a team toward a common goal is a very natural experience. Why such a drastic difference for Generation Y? It is because of the way Gen Y has been socialized. Remember their parents were in mommy-to-be classes with their soon-to-be group of play-date friends before they were even born. Generation Y has essentially been working in teams their entire lives, so their preference at work is to collaborate with others. Solitude and working independently can feel unnatural for this generation.

Relationships: comparison between generation Y and other generations

Generation Y	Preceding Generations
Started socializing at an early age before they could talk.	Emphasis on establishing friendships outside of the family did not occur until preschool or kindergarten.
Emphasis was placed on extra-curricular group activities.	Less emphasis on extra-curricular activities and when they occurred they were usually school based or community-based. Individual extra-curricular activities (piano lessons) held same importance as group activities.
Taught that it is okay to speak frankly in social situations.	In social situations, taught that there are things you discuss with your friends and things you do not.
Early adulthood: family obligations were/are the priority.	Early adulthood: getting married later in life resulting in increased time with friends and having children later in life resulting in more time with spouses and friends before becoming parents.
Relationships begin and thrive through face-to-face contact, and these same relationships can be maintained through phone conversations and e-mail; however, rarely does a new friendship result from a digital relationship.	Relationships can begin and thrive without face-to-face contact via digital communication.
Will leave a job if socialization needs are not met.	Are not likely to leave a job due to socialization needs.

Diversity within + exposure to a wide range of diverse lifestyles = acceptance of others

In this country Generation Y is a diverse group. Approximately one-third are members of minority groups. They have been exposed to various cultures and lifestyles and at the very least have experienced some form of global exposure through various Websites and television shows. Many members of Generation Y have friends who are from various backgrounds or lead differing lifestyles. In addition, Gen Y was probably the first generation to be raised in a time period where there were less noticeable barriers to an integrated culture. This is not to say that Gen Y is not aware of racism or prejudice or does not display it, but they are a generation that reaped the benefits of their parent's protests for civil rights regardless of age, gender, race, sexual orientation, and mental or medical health status. Consequently, this generation brings this appreciation for those who are different from themselves to the workplace. Remember, they grew up learning that each person is unique and each person is different and special. They have both personally and through media (for example, television, movies, books, and music) been exposed to a wide range of diverse lifestyles, customs, disabilities, and differences more so than other generations. Generation Y not only embraces differences, they tend to motivate and expect others to do the same.

What has also contributed to their tendency to be more accepting of diverse backgrounds is this generation's exposure to social networking sites. On these sites, your friends can become your friend's friend, and in fact if two or more of your friends have a friend in common, you are notified that there may be a friend you might want to invite to be one of your "friends." The fact that these sites are free and the Internet is widely accessible means that these "friendships" have become very egalitarian. Poor, wealthy, young, old, unemployed or barely working, students, office workers, and so on can all socialize without socioeconomic status being a factor. This results in a conglomeration of many friends and friends of friends who may share different values, foundations, and/ or life experiences. This has resulted in an increased acceptance of diversity.

Generation Y's large social range: awareness of the people and social causes around them

In addition to diversity awareness, social awareness has been a priority for this generation as a whole. They are one of the most socially aware generations, and feeling as though they are helping others has consistently been a part of their personal mission. Although we used to intimately know our smaller communities based on where we lived, Generation Y looks at the larger community well beyond their own backyard and neighborhoods mainly because they are globally connected through technology. This global connection fosters a cultural ideology reflecting social justice, environmental concern, and global community. Engaging in social missions has become a form of socialization for this generation. More specifically, networking sites encourage members to have friends join causes to raise awareness or money to help others. It is not uncommon to receive numerous invitations to join a cause to help others every day. Generation Y may not truly be philanthropists, for example, there are several causes you can join on Facebook and they become buttons or bumper stickers of support. One can "show off" causes they "support" or want others to see they think are important without actually having to do anything. However, for this generation, being involved and feeling like they are helping others is a priority.

Three advantages of Generation Y's relationship style

"The meeting of two personalities is like the contact of two chemical substances; if there is any reaction, both are transformed."

—Carl Jung (1875–1961)

Who is a team player? Gen Y is!

Interpersonal relationships are a priority for Generation Y. Always able to have instantaneous connections with others due to digital media, Generation Y relies on social relationships. They are naturals in groups or teams. This generation is used to working/playing well with others, and they have been doing so since the beginning of their lives. Because they are natural team players, placing this group in their natural habitat or setting will help them thrive. This is true as long as it is not impacted by corporate "pollutants" (for example, micromanaging, poor leadership, lack of vision, and so on) or interpersonal differences with co-workers (that is, coworkers not working within Gen Y's expectations, telling them what to do or how to do it, and so on).

A leader says:

"Gen Y's are team players. But, they want to be placed in a team with others who they feel are just as smart as they are. They do not do well in environments where they view their colleagues as less capable."

Douglas J. Zogby, CPCU, president,

Got Game! Consulting

Real relationships—not just work relationships

This is a generation where work/life integration is demanded and relationships are vital components of this. Without solid relationships at work, especially with one's boss, integration fails, motivation decreases, and loyalty suffers. You will rarely hear a Gen Y say, "Oh, this is just a work friend" with the meaning that it is someone they know through work and socialize with the majority of the time, if not exclusively, at work. When the preceding generations say "work friend" as opposed to "friend" they are using it to differentiate between an associate they did not have the choice to meet and a close friend. This is not to say that individuals from other generations do not have wonderful friends whom they met through work; however, it probably took much longer then it takes Generation Y for that friendship to develop from "work friends" to actually spending time outside of the office together.

It may be common that when a Gen Y leaves a company they will maintain, at a similarly intense level, the friendships they made while there. This tends to be a big difference across generations, because Gen Y values connection via digital means as much as a connection via face-to-face time. This allows for a "virtual water cooler" experience where friendships can be maintained regardless of the nine-to-five contact.

A leader says:

"Generation Y's are very loathsome to screw someone over because they have such a sense of community. There are virtually no cliques, no politics, because they all feel that they are part of a team."

Kent Lewis, president,

Anvil Media, Inc.

Acceptance for all

Generation Y has been exposed to and taught the importance of accepting diversity throughout their lives. This exposure has developed a strong generational social conscience and broadening of awareness and acceptance of others. This generation, as a whole, does not suffer from the same prejudices that other generations have suffered from because they were raised in a different cultural zeitgeist. When prejudice does exist for members of Generation Y, although it may be with the same intensity as other generations, it is often hidden. Same sex parenting, equal opportunities for women, minorities, and individuals with disabilities has created an open-minded generation that demands global awareness in the workplace. Because social awareness and care of others is important to this generation, they care about how their companies give back to society and the community.

A leader says:

"My company has always given back to the community in the form of fundraising events, donating to causes and producing pro-bono work to benefit a cause. What I have found interesting is that my Gen Y employees show more interest in wanting part of their work to include these community activities. They are the ones that immediately jump on the design projects that are pro-bono for a community cause."

R. Tillery, owner and creative director,
Graphic Design Company

Three challenges of Generation Y's relationship style

"Everything that irritates us about others can lead us to an understanding of ourselves."

—Carl Jung (1875–1961)

One second—let me just send this text first

One disadvantage of this generation's social focus and their need for work-life integration, is that the Tweeting, Facebooking, blogging, and texting, never ends and can be disruptive during the workday. Sure, they are better at multitasking than most, and allowing them social access during the workday is recommended, but sometimes their need for social connection can interfere with productivity. The goal is to help them strike a good balance. Provide them with the ability and resources to remain connected, but also help them learn to manage their time effectively.

A leader says:

"There was a Gen Y employee that worked for me that would literally sign into her Gmail account in the morning and not sign out until she was done with her day. Her work performance was poor and she was constantly behind on her deadlines. Her colleagues were often complaining about her performance. I warned her several times and finally made up a lie telling her that I have a monitoring system in place with the hope that she would cut down her socializing time during work hours. It didn't work and we had to let her go."

Kent Lewis, president,
Anvil Media, Inc.

"Boss, I was so drunk last night," and other things you never wanted to hear about

Because Generation Y grew up being BFF with their peers, parents, and teachers, this has transferred into the workplace and changed workplace formality. This is a generation that was taught to say it like it is and that anything and everything is appropriate to talk about with anyone and everyone. This is not always such a bad thing. However, when a Gen Y employee brags to the boss about how drunk he or she was the night before (and then expects the boss to take it easy on them for the day), the old days of formality and respect are deeply missed. In addition, most workplaces are not ready, have no desire to, or are not capable of letting go of the traditional ways of conducting business and workplace relationships. It can be quite frustrating when the newest employees are demanding an overhaul in how the talk is talked and the walk is walked. These demands often clash with the traditional way of doing business and often cause multiple problems in inter-generational relationships.

Did this really happen? Yes!

Jill Ferguson, a college professor at Notre Dame University, commented on the outspoken and bold qualities of Generation Y. She stated, "Gen Y is not afraid to say what they think and often do not separate their personal and work relationship boundaries." She reported that recently one of her 20-year-old male students was 20 minutes late to her class and when he arrived he said to her in front of the class, "Sorry I was late. I was having sex with my girlfriend."

Loyalty reprised

A Generation Y employee may join an organization because a friend works there, or remain on a job because of their social connections, so many easily rationalize leaving a company if their social connections change within the workplace, or if an opportunity presents itself that allows them to feel more socially connected elsewhere. This again brings into question the issue of loyalty, company retention, and engagement strategies. Because Gen Y is connected to people, not necessarily organizations, they can be more easily swayed in their organizational commitments based on perceived social loyalties. The days of working for The Company may be gone. There has been a dramatic shift toward leaving an organization if one's trusted colleague or boss leaves.

HR chimes in:

"Generation Y travel in packs, so when one leaves it is not just the loss of that one employee, but also the loss of the people they pull away with them."

Mary Hobbes, VP of human resources,
Large Pharmaceutical Company

The takeaways so far...

If you remember nothing else, take away the following:

> For Generation Y, constant communication with friends and family is expected, regardless of work responsibilities.

> Solid relationships with those they work for and with are a priority.

> They are used to socializing together and prefer to work together on shared goals.

› Diversity, social awareness, and helping others has always been a part of life for this generation, and they expect this to be honored by their companies.

You can use Gen Y's relationship style to your advantage by:

› Utilizing their group social abilities and team player attitudes.

› Understanding the power that relationships with coworkers and supervisors have with regard to individual and overall company success.

› Remembering that Generation Y is accepting of others and cares about the missions and community/global messages of the companies where they work.

Watch out for Gen Y's tendency to:

› Value communication with their friends over work responsibilities.

› Tell more personal information than you may be ready to hear.

› Leave a company because a valued colleague/boss/friend left.

Now it's time to take some action. Here are the coaching solutions that we recommend to enhance the positives and manage the negatives of Generation Y's relationship style.

Coaching solutions: building on strengths and addressing the challenges

The importance that Generation Y places on relationships has created several opportunities within the workplace, and, therefore, it is beneficial to understand how this generation relates to others differently than preceding generations. Harnessing these strengths for the benefit of the organization, as well as utilizing coaching strategies to help minimize the problems that arise from their unique relationship styles will help develop your Gen Y employees' leadership potential.

No-brainer coaching solutions

CS1: Staffing the "relationship-building" social committee

The creation of social committees can benefit the individual, the team, and the organization. Because Generation Y tends to value the social aspects of work and benefit from praise and recognition, offer a role of leadership through staffing a social committee. This can be done by having them lead and organize appropriate social committees, maybe even as the social chair. Ideas for team social committees can include the following:

> Individuals of the team put money into a pot and the company can match it for quarterly social events outside of the office.

> Have an opportunities and accomplishments board that acknowledges successes of individual team members, or teams and provides information about different opportunities for the team (and individuals).

> Plan bimonthly or monthly lunches for the team where only non-work related conversations are allowed.

> E-mail recognition when projects are completed.

> Annual celebrations with company and team contributions.

> MVT (Most Valuable Team) trophies, which can be given out on a weekly, monthly, or yearly basis.

Team-building exercises and retreats can occur within a more informal and less time- and financial-consuming manner then you might think. A Friday afternoon lunch or happy hour, a company baseball or bowling team, a book group, or potluck lunches are all examples of team building activities that cost a little but go a long way.

Why it works

For all generations, strong workplace relationships, work/life integration, and fun are imperative to enhancing company loyalty and productivity. Making work a place where people look forward to coming to because of their relationships, as well as enjoyment of the tasks begins with putting the right structures in place to allow for both to occur. Research has consistently shown that good relationships with colleagues aids in the enhancement of loyalty to a company and makes it difficult for employees to leave, because they also have to leave their trusted community. Recognizing this is imperative to strengthening organizational culture, and also demonstrates corporate emotional competence. Although many companies already have social committees, the idea here is to recognize the social strengths of the Y generation and put them in positions of authority within the social committee. Companies, small and large, have found great success with this approach.

Idea into action

One company had their social committee staffed by their youngest employees, and had them take turns organizing and running the various social events. They laughed at how difficult it was in the beginning to not talk about work-related topics at their organized "no-work" lunches. The social committee put whistles on the table with instructions to blow the whistle when someone spoke about work and then ask that person a question that was non-work related. The company talked about how much fun it was, and that when they came back to work they felt more connected and more energized. Not only did everyone seem to enjoy the activities, but the Gen Y's that were in charge gained a sense of pride in their ability to bring everyone together and create opportunities for people to connect on a personal level.

CS2: One big happy work family

When we enjoy who we are working with, productivity is increased. On the other hand, when personal conflicts arise at work or there is general dislike, the work environment can quickly become a gossip festival where there is more talk about, "he said, she said" than "this and that are now completed." Positive social relationships at work are of particular importance to Generation Y. Think of making a shift from socializing when there is time, to creating a culture that holds relationships in the workplace as a priority. These important relationships can be fostered in a number of ways.

For large companies with several locations nationally or internationally, it would be beneficial to get everyone together in one location, maybe once a year, similar to a big family reunion. Although this is a financial investment, it is an important one, especially if there is a high level of daily contact between coworkers in different company locations. The "work/family reunion" does not have to be an isolated event. It could be a part of other business that is currently on the company agenda. If a large company-wide event seems impossible, we recommend pulling together mini reunions between teams, so face-to-face relationship building and idea sharing can occur.

For smaller companies, smaller-scale activities could be arranged that focus on creating regular opportunities for coworkers to get together inside and outside of work hours (that is, from the traditional scheduled happy hours to take-the-coworker-you-would-like-to-get-to-know-better-out-to-lunch-day). In addition, because it is easier to pull together company-wide events for businesses that are smaller in size, we recommend holding a few events a year to enhance relationship and morale building. However, everyone does the holiday party and company picnic. Think outside the box to really develop teamwork and engage your Gen Y's (and other generations). Examples of unique company-wide events include: a company-wide fundraising event, a bowling tournament to raise money for a charity, a company-wide volunteering day where everyone works for the same organization to accomplish a goal together, or "the company Olympics" where teams train together for certain events throughout the year and compete against other teams (not only promoting team-building, but promoting health and wellness through physical activity to ultimately reduce healthcare costs).

Why it works

Very simply, the values that a company espouses impacts the employees that choose to work there. If a company values relationship-building and creates opportunities for this to be expressed, then the employees are going to be positively impacted. Ultimately, the company will likely experience increased loyalty, better teamwork, and improved productivity. Strong relationships within a company impact worker satisfaction, and thus, the bottom line. An added perk is that a company that develops interpersonal relationships will do better recruiting and retaining talented Gen Y's.

Important note: You will find that some of your employees are not interested in social activities. Take a moment to check if their resistance is due to anxiety, stress outside of work, or another issue before judging their lack of interest. Checking in with employees who seem unwilling paves the way for an opportunity to understand more about that employee, and possibly help them overcome a barrier.

Idea into action

The owner of a small architecture firm was trying to find a way to build and foster employee relationships. He decided to try "work family" lunches once a week. He loved to cook, so it was easy for him to prepare a family style lunch. Everyone was asked to join to eat together and there were no expectations set. He admitted that during the first "work/family" lunch, some of his employees appeared a little uncomfortable wondering what his motives were. However, by the second and third "work family" lunch, employees were looking forward to the lunches. In fact, eventually those people who enjoyed cooking started signing up to be the "work/family" lunch chef for a week.

Brainer coaching solutions

CS3: Building teams Generation Y style

Teamwork can contribute to a company's success. Teams can accomplish more in less time, they have built in sounding boards, and they allow for task delegation based on people's strengths. Generation Y is a generation of natural team players and they prefer to work in team formats. However, because of their work tendencies, expectations, and demands, there are many reasons that teams could fail. This coaching solution focuses on harnessing the strengths they bring to teams and minimizing the potential obstacles of Generation Y's contributions to teams based on their work preferences.

Gen Y team problems and solutions

1. **Problem:** Desire to have guidance and support from top management.

   Solution: Elect a team liaison to act as the point person or "squad leader" whose role it is to communicate between the team and upper management. Consider offering this position to a Gen Y team member, because they crave leadership roles and communication opportunities with their bosses.

2. **Problem:** Only the loudest voices are heard. Due to their sense of entitlement and frankness with sharing their ideas, chances are it is your Gen Y employee who is speaking the loudest.

   Solution: Have brainstorming sessions where everyone thinks individually and then each person shares his or her thoughts through the use of a moderator.

3. **Problem:** Rewards are given for individual accomplishments and not the accomplishments of the group. Gen Y is motivated by external rewards, and if individual rewards are given to others and not to them, they will be the first to notice and may have difficulty with it.

   Solution: Provide rewards that are group based, not individual based.

4. **Problem:** Although Gen Y shows initiative with regard to coming up with creative ideas and solutions, they often lack followthrough and accountability for their work, especially when a mistake is made or they do not know what to do next.

   Solution: Be sure that group tasks are delegated into parts, with each team member being held responsible for their individual task. Also be clear with expectations for the task and clearly define due dates.

5. **Problem:** Lack of awareness of individual team members' talents and strengths. Gen Y prefers to work in teams with individuals who they respect. They tend to become disgruntled when they believe that others they are working with do not have their same

skill level. It is not necessarily because people "aren't smart enough" or "as capable," it is simply that the team is not aware of each others' talents and potential obstacles.

Solution: Hire a consultant to do a team assessment. The consultant will help your team gain insight into the team's functioning as a whole, as well as the individual team member's strengths and needs. Armed with this knowledge, teams can function at a significantly higher level. We recommend investing in this type of assessment the minute a team is formed in your company.

Gen Y team strengths and enhancements

1. **Strength:** They prefer team and social environments.

   Enhancement: Because Gen Y prefers this style of work let them be the team lead. If this is not possible because of seniority issues, let them have a defined role on the team, such as team moderator or team liaison).

2. **Strength:** Open to diversity and differences within the group.

   Enhancement: After a the consultant has completed the team assessment, put a Gen Y employee in charge of reminding the group of the results of that assessment (that is, strengths and obstacles of the team and the individuals) to bring focus back to the group, serving the function of a team moderator.

3. **Strength:** They think outside of the box with novel ideas and tend to be frank when sharing their thoughts.

   Enhancement: Listen to them, even if you are shocked by how the message is being relayed. Help redirect them if necessary, but listen to their ideas.

Big-brainer coaching solutions

CS4: The team milieu-nnium

Because Gen Y's are naturals when it comes to teamwork, we suggest, if possible, creating a team environment, or what we like to call, "team milieu." Creating a workplace culture that nurtures teams can provide positive business outcomes. When creating a team milieu from scratch you need to make sure that you build in the necessary features to promote and encourage success.

Shrinkwrapped

The word milieu *has often been used when describing the impact of one's social environment on positive changes in one's behavior.*

Teams thrive when they are provided with the following structure and opportunities:

> ‣ Time to have meetings to discuss shared goals, planning, and processes.
> ‣ Planned benchmarks for celebrations, so the team as a whole can work toward goals.
> ‣ Intra-team mentorship opportunities.
> ‣ Creative brainstorming sessions.
> ‣ Making technological resources available to account for team member's flexible schedules and preferred work styles.
> ‣ Healthy competition among different teams in your milieu to enhance inter-team cohesiveness, collaboration, and productivity.

When creating the team milieu, beware of a common problem associated with reduced team productivity: group think.

Shrinkwrapped

Groupthink, a concept identified by Irving Janis, describes flawed decision-making that can occur within groups. The problematic decision making happens when critical examination of alternatives and outside expert opinions are avoided, because the team is already convinced that their decisions are correct due to group cohesiveness.

Signs that your team is operating under Groupthink include:

1. The group begins to rationalize their poor and ineffective decisions.
2. A team that appears to be unreceptive to outside forces.
3. A team that stops allowing inter-member dissent.

Solutions to fix a team that is operating under Groupthink:

1. Assign impartial leaders to the team
2. Require that the team report their proposed solutions to a larger team or group.
3. Elect or hire an outside expert to sit in on the team decision-making process.

4. Require the team to come up with a few solutions to a problem and then present these to a another team for feedback and the final decision.

In addition to being aware of groupthink, pay attention to another common problem associated with reduced team cohesiveness and productivity: social loafing.

Shrinkwrapped

Social Loafing, proposed by Max Ringelmann (1913), describes the tendency for people to slack off or not carry their weight when working in teams or groups where their contributions to the final product cannot be identified. Often when there are two individuals working on a project each person is likely to do 50 percent of the work. However, according to social loafing theory, the more people involved in a project, the more likely it is that one or two people will do the majority of the work and the others will loaf.

Signs that your team is operating with Social Loafing:

1. People on teams can identify the loafers pretty quickly.
2. You start hearing others complain about the loafers.
3. The individuals carrying the weight of the team start to burn out as evidenced by reduced productivity or medical/mental health complaints.

Solutions to fix a team that is operating with Social Loafers:

1. Assign individual tasks and responsibilities with clear deadlines and defined expectations.
2. Make sure that everyone on the team knows that during their performance evaluation period, which we recommend having quarterly, they will be evaluated by other members of the team.

Why it works

Generation Y's preferred work style involves a team approach. They are also a generation that needs growth and mentoring opportunities. Working within a team milieu will assist this generation with learning how to work well across generations, and provide opportunities for relationship building, which is imperative for retaining and engaging your Gen Y employees. Further, teamwork can be an incredible asset to the overall organization because of its inherent benefits of enhanced relationships, enhanced productivity, and improved idea creation. As a result of the foundation of solid relationships, loyalty will increase.

Coaching solutions simplified

Coaching Solution 1

Title: Staffing the "relationship-building" social committee.

Purpose: To give Gen Y an opportunity for a leadership position offering work opportunities that allows them to promote fluidity between work and life.

Outcome: Generation Y retention and engagement, leadership building opportunity, and relationship building.

Coaching Solution 2

Title: One big happy work family.

Purpose: To create opportunities for important relationship building company events.

Outcome: Relationship building and increased morale.

Coaching Solution 3

Title: Building teams generation Y style.

Purpose: To hone the strengths and minimize the weaknesses of Gen Y's team work tendencies.

Outcome: Relationship building, increased productivity, increased self-awareness, increased awareness, and understanding of others.

Coaching Solution 4

Title: The team milieu-nnium.

Purpose: To create a team environment that promotes success.

Outcome: Intergenerational relationship building, increased productivity, enhanced loyalty, and company cohesiveness.

——Chapter 8——

Managing Gen Y and Their Moods: Drugs, Attention, and Quarter-Life Crises

"When written in Chinese, the word crisis *is composed of two characters: one represents danger, and the other represents opportunity."*

—John F. Kennedy (1917–1963)

"My experience working with college students has been varied. Ten years ago I treated students for problems such as depression, anxiety, and academic problems. Although each case was different and required varied strategies, reaching out for support from friends and family members was often a common coping mechanism. Most students understood what that meant and how to basically go about doing that. In the past several years, the same concept almost seems completely foreign to current college students. These days, most students communicate with others through text messages, IM, e-mails, or Facebook. None of these involve face-to-face contact, which is why I think the students I see today do not understand what it means to talk with friends and family when they are emotionally troubled. Furthermore, this may also be why even little crises seem so overwhelming to them. So, when a student experiences a relationship break up, it is not uncommon to hear them say they have no hope of life getting better and no idea what to do. I just don't remember hearing this 10 years ago."

K. Scott, PhD, psychologist,
College Counseling Center

This is the first generation in which psychiatric medication use was a common rather than an unusual phenomenon. If they were not prescribed a psychiatric medication themselves, some of their friends were. These medications are often sustained into their adult life as they continue to struggle focusing their attention and managing their moods. Often those in management are not aware of how many employees are on medication. However, the upside is that Generation Y was brought up having an awareness of how they feel and are able to express themselves, even if this often occurs through digital formats, such as blogs, where little response is given back to them about their thoughts and feelings.

Emotional expression (managed by medication) coupled with finding out that they might not be everything and anything they were told they could be has created a bit of a downfall. This may be the reason why the "quarter-life crisis" has became a common occurrence. In response to these quarter life crises, along with their ability to speak up and speak out, they are also a generation more likely to seek out professional help and to talk openly about their relationship conflicts at home and in the workplace. They are also more apt to share their feelings of stress or panic about where they are in their lives, their feelings of defeat, and/or their disappointment in what life has thrown their way. However, it is important to note that they tend to do so in monologue fashion rather than through connected conversations with others. Boomers and older Gen Xers were raised to cope with and handle stressors by themselves, or by talking to friends and family, rather than seeking out professional help. It was only recently that having a "shrink" has become accepted, which has been perpetuated by the needs of Gen Y (and younger Gen X).

Back to the (psychological) basics

Who do I want to be when I grow up?

In the past, the process of solidifying one's identity occurred during late adolescence. It was a natural developmental period when teenagers began the separation process from their parents, found more influence and direction from their peers, and found their own ways led by the values and morals instilled from their upbringing. However, a shift has been happening. Although teenagers are still seeking separation from their parents to form their own identity, with one foot in the door and one foot out, this process is lasting longer and longer (or reemerging) into what used to be a time called adulthood.

Shrinkwrapped

Erik Erikson, a psychologist who developed a theory of psychosocial development, discussed adolescence (ages 12–17) as a time when one emerges with an understanding and solid belief in who they are (Identity) or they become confused with who they are (Role Confusion). This is also a time in development when it was theorized that adolescents separate from their family of origin and re-develop an adult relationship with their parents. Erikson developed his theory in 1950, and while the stages of human development are valid today, it is easy to see that times have changed and the stage of identity versus role confusion now happens much later in life.

There are many reasons that the developmental processes of childhood are prolonged today. Higher college enrollments, marrying later, less financial responsibilities, and extended parenting past the age of 18 are a few of the reasons that Gen Y's take longer to figure out who they want to be when they grow up. So when do you actually become grown up? When the Veteran generation were children, school was a luxury, not a priority. Often kids who were growing up during the Veteran generation had to leave school to work in order to help sustain the family. Obviously the times have changed, allowing children to be children. However, it seems like society has shifted to quite an extreme by preventing kids (even post-college-age adults) from growing up. The undeclared major has become quite popular, as has taking a few months off to travel the world, delaying careers to teach abroad, and postponing responsibility by "shacking up with the 'rents till I figure it out." The million-dollar question is, "What is everyone trying to figure out?"

Delaying adulthood into the mid- to late 20s means that a majority of the youngest employees in the workforce are still engaging in the process of becoming adults. This also results in delayed development or underdevelopment of coping skills for handling the stress and struggles of daily life and work responsibilities.

Shrinkwrapped

A coping mechanism is either an unconscious or learned tool or strategy that we use to handle major or minor stressors and/or emotions. Some coping mechanisms can be healthy, (for example, going for a run after a stressful day at work, or journaling our feelings) and some can be detrimental to our health (for example, smoking cigarettes or drinking alcohol when stressed).

What is often observed in the workplace is that many Generation Y employees have unrealistic expectations about work, about their positions, and about where they are going. What has also been delayed is their ability to take responsibility for their actions. Instead what managers often hear are excuses, excuses, excuses.

Premature quasi-existential crisis (PQEC)

A premature mid-life crisis, or a quarter-life crisis, has become a frequent occurrence among 20-somethings. We feel that the Premature Quasi-Existential Crisis (PQEC) is the best term to describe what we have observed Gen Y experiencing. We call it the PQEC because it is a time in life where decisions that were made earlier are challenged, and thoughts of, "What's my purpose (in this career)?" "Why am I here (in this career)?" are contemplated without a focus on the purpose and meaning of life in general, as is the case in existential crises. In an existential crisis, someone experiences psychological discomfort when grappling with questions regarding existence and the meaning of life. In PQEC a person contemplates their career and there is often psychological discomfort experienced with the fear of "I haven't made it yet," "my opportunities to make it are dwindling," "my managers are not seeing my full potential," and so on. The PQEC has become so common that it may be appropriate to say that a new developmental stage is emerging right between the ages of "young college student" and "Crap, I'm an adult." PQEC is a time of confusion, disappointment, fear, and searching for a direction and an identity.

When this occurs, everything feels like it is falling apart. For the most part, Gen Yers have been known to have a difficult time coping with problems when they occur, so when the problem that they are trying to handle involves the overall questions of, "Who am I," "Why am I working here," and "This position is a waste of my time and skill, why am I doing this?," they may appear to engage in rash decision-making and behaviors (that is, exaggerated emotional outbursts, leaving a job unexpectedly, and taking a new direction with their career or life). These quarter-life crises can be so overwhelming, caused by normal life realizations and relatively normal growing pains, that a revolution has occurred where everyone seems to have a shrink and everyone is aware of the newest psychiatric medication to dull or "cure" what sometimes may just be normal developmental growth periods.

Less stigma, better detection, and applying diagnoses left and right for unwanted behaviors

Across the world, rates of children who are prescribed psychiatric drugs have risen throughout the past several years. The good news is that the social stigma associated with mental health or stress-related problems has diminished. In the past, if someone had a mental health disorder, people would talk about it in a whisper. Today, having ADHD, depression, or anxiety is accepted. How did this happen? Are there really more children and young adults with ADHD, depression, and anxiety, or are we as a society trying to find reasons and explanations for behaviors that are not easily redirected into more desired behaviors. For example, let's look at some of the symptoms of ADHD: shortened attention span, easily distracted, not always thinking before acting, lots of energy, squirming and fidgeting, and/or interrupting others. Do any of these symptoms appear to be symptoms of being a child? So, how many children are medicated for ADHD or labeled as ADHD for the rest of their lives because they were acting like the children they were at the time? Of course we are not saying that this diagnosis is not real, without a doubt it absolutely is, and it can be truly devastating and difficult to manage. But the percentage of children diagnosed with ADHD and the percentage of children prescribed Ritalin and Adderal has drastically increased so much so that either there must be something in the water, or ADHD is being over-diagnosed.

So, why is there a higher incidence of diagnoses being assigned and medications being prescribed? Some of the reasons include: Children and young adults have limited coping skills leading to maladjustment, and there are better tools to understand, diagnose, and treat problems. Although there is increased tolerance and acceptance for seeking help for mental health problems, there is a decreased tolerance for dealing with mental health symptoms so that medication/help is sought immediately if things are not going as planned. There are obviously advantages and disadvantages to this phenomenon. The stigma of mental health problems has been weakened, however a diagnosis (whether warranted or not) is often applied to unwanted behavior. We have become an overmedicated nation where people pop a pill to sleep, to concentrate, to feel less sad, to manage their inability to manage, to boost their energy, to lose weight, to gain weight, and so on. This double-edged sword has created more comfort with the mental health field and awareness of mental health issues as a whole, but has also allowed "disability," whether feigned or real, to be used as an excuse not to operate and function merely at an inadequate level.

This generation has grown up normalizing mental health problems, and society in general is labeling behaviors quickly without a thorough evaluation. By quickly diagnosing "the problem" without thorough consideration of normal behaviors or underlying causes: parents, doctors, and Gen Ys themselves are inadvertently ignoring the real problem, which is that this generation has not had the opportunity to develop effective coping skills. Many Gen Ys are ill-equipped to deal with day-to-day responsibilities, stressors, and normal developmental growing pains. Sure, everyone's problems are unique and at times in life each one of us can easily become overwhelmed. However, for Generation Y, basic coping mechanisms seem to be severely underdeveloped and this creates multiple challenges in the workplace. So, although professional help can provide opportunities to foster those essential skills, it is a whole life issue not just a mental health one.

Three advantages of Generation Y's psychological awareness

"Let us not look back in anger or forward in fear, but around in awareness."
—James Thurber (1894–1961)

Extreme emotional awareness

This generation is significantly more emotionally aware (not necessarily emotionally intelligent) than any generation before. They were taught the words, meaning, and how to identify emotions at a very young age. They were encouraged to "use their words" instead of behaviors to describe how they are feeling. Not only were they allowed and expected to speak their minds, they were encouraged to air their problems, concerns, fears, and weaknesses. Increased awareness of mental health problems, the self-help movement and wellness initiatives have created a generation that is comfortable with their emotions and problems. Although they are able to identify their problems they do not necessarily know what to do about how they are feeling. However, they will share with the world (and their bosses) how they are feeling, so there is rarely any wonder of what a Gen Y is going/working through at any given moment.

A leader says:

Erica Lui, a consultant for a PR and marketing firm told us, "I'm amazed and sometimes appalled at how easy it is for this generation to talk about their personal problems with such candor. I'm glad I know what's going on but sometimes it's a little too much information for me."

Open to asking for help

Because this generation was encouraged to express themselves, they have been more open to, and more able to ask for, assistance. They are not afraid to ask questions (repeatedly if necessary) or to seek advice and counseling if they do not know the answer to something. They will also ask for help when they feel that they cannot independently work through something. They are aware of how they are feeling and look to others to assist them with "what to do about how they are feeling." This can be a positive aspect at work, as they will check in and look for guidance rather than go full steam ahead in the wrong direction.

A leader says:

"I've noticed with this generation that I am constantly bombarded with questions of why, how, and what should I do. Although it is time consuming, I try to see this as a great thing because I can at least understand where they are having road blocks."

R. Tillery, owner and creative director,
Graphic Design Company

I'm okay with me and I'm okay with you

This generation is very diverse and relativistic. Because this generation tends to be more socially conscious and active in social missions, they are also more open to others with disabilities and differences. With inclusive classrooms, environments where everyone is a winner and volunteerism on the rise, this generation is more apt to be socially inclusive, understanding, and empathetic to the plight of others. They are honest with who they are and okay with other people being who they are.

> **HR chimes in:**
> *"We have to give diversity training for all of our employees at our company. Gen Y seems to be on top of so many issues when it comes to diversity and openness. They really bring a unique perspective to our company."*
> *Elizabeth Bradley, HR manager,*
> *Financial Services Company*

Three challenges of Generation Y's psychological awareness

"We don't see things as they are, we see them as we are."

—Anaïs Nin (1903–1977)

Excuses, excuses, excuses and more excuses

Because this generation has been raised on Ritalin, Prozac, and therapy, they are more likely than other generations to use their "emotional issues" as an excuse to function or behave in a less than acceptable way. I'm bored, I'm sad, I'm tired, I'm manic, I have this life crisis or that life crisis happening, and I can't concentrate because I forgot to take my meds this morning are excuses for poor performance. In the past, these excuses would never be tolerated in the workplace. Today, however, they are common, and sometimes acceptable reasons why someone "can't" perform to the best of their ability on any given day. Ys have difficulty discerning "real" problems from problems that should not affect work performance and productivity. In addition, Gen Y tends to openly admit their problems, but do not necessarily take responsibility for them. Rather, they are often seeking sympathy rather than feedback on how to make a change. The Boomer generation works with many of their life issues that arise, whereas Gen Y is much more likely to have even what most would consider smaller life issues (that is, relationship breakups, fender-bender car accidents, argument with significant others) interrupt their ability to work, with the expectation that their employers should and will understand and make accommodations for them.

A leader says:

"I often hear the phrase, 'I just can't' or 'I'm having a crisis' coming out of the mouths of Gen Yers. The thing is, once you say 'can't' or 'crisis' your back is up against a wall as a manager. If someone says they are having a 'crisis,' how can you hold them accountable for their behavior?"

Stevie Ray, executive director,

Stevie Ray's Improv Company

Career existential crisis—backfired

When observing Gen Y you may see that many in this generation are experiencing PQEC. Freak-outs often result in job-hopping, unrealistic expectations, and dramatic emotional experiences. When one "freaks out" it is a sign that their coping mechanisms have failed, resulting in a crisis. The problem is, these poor coping skills are often in reaction to normal growing pains, which accompany typical life stressors that go hand in hand with being an adult. This generation has higher expectations for where they should be at a younger age. The consequences of the self-inflation movement (for example, inability to tolerate failure or mistakes) tend to perpetuate their freak-outs. The quarter- life crisis can be prolonged by their ability to fall back on their parents' dime and live at home for a while to figure things out.

Did this really happen? Yes!

"I had this Gen Y employee call out of work for several days after her boyfriend of the past years broke up with her. She told me that she was just too sad to work and would do some of her work from home if I thought that would be necessary. When I challenged her about this as a reason for missing work, she totally flipped out on me and never came back to work."

J. Joyce, marketing director,

Large retail chain

I can tell you how I feel, but if you don't tell me how you are feeling I might not notice

Generation Y is extremely effective at identifying and expressing how they are feeling. They are also open and accepting of others who express their current downfalls and disabilities. However, if you do not share with them how you are feeling and what you are experiencing then they might not realize it for themselves. They may become confused and misinterpret your actions as a direct reflection of their behavior. Although it is common for Generation Y to designate feeling words to bad moods or bad days, this is not common for the other generations who usually just continue to work right through the day and explore or analyze feelings later or never. This is a foreign concept to Generation Y, and therefore they may not be able to pick up on how their boss or others are feeling unless it is told to them in a straightforward manner. Instead, if the boss is just having a bad day (and not necessarily voicing their bad day to their staff), a Gen Y employee may think that their boss is acting that way because of something that the Gen Y did or because of some other incorrect reason. Again, this generation has good emotional awareness when it comes to their own emotions, but tends to be somewhat self-focused. Others emotional experiences are often misinterpreted and taken personally and can often impact performance.

A leader says:

"When I'm having a bad day at work, I have a tendency to close the door, be a little uncommunicative, and perhaps give off a 'leave me alone vibe.' I manage a group of Gen Y's and have noticed that this doesn't work at all. In fact, on the days that I'm having a bad day, they tend to have bad days. After looking at this, I realized that I have to be better at communicating that 'I'm just having a bad day', so they get where I am coming from and can go on with what they have to do."
Felicia Smith, VP of human resources,
Large medical equipment company

The takeaways so far...

If you remember nothing else, take away the following:

› There appears to be an longer identity developmental phase between adolescence and adulthood.

› Many members of Generation Y have underdeveloped coping skills for handling the stress and struggles of daily life and work responsibilities.

› When high and often unrealistic career expectations are not met and a Gen Y starts to question who they are and what type of work they want to do a Premature Quasi-Existential Crisis (PQEC) may occur.

You can use Gen Y's tendency toward psychological awareness to your advantage by:

> Observing their high emotional awareness and emotional expressions as they are able to tell you exactly how they feel.

> Realizing their openness to ask for help and guidance.

> Appreciating them for their social inclusiveness and under standing of those that are different from them.

Watch out for Gen Y's tendency to:

> Use emotional issues/responses to life situations as excuses in the workplace.

> Have unrealistic expectations and dramatic emotional expressions in conjunction with the PQEC.

> Not be observant of your bad mood or bad day, sometimes taking it personally unless you specifically share with them how you are feeling.

Now it's time to take some action. Here are the coaching solutions that we recommend to enhance the positives and manage the negatives of Generation Y's psychological awareness.

Coaching solutions: building on strengths and addressing the challenges

Generation Y brings unique strengths and challenges into the workplace due to the increased time period of their identity development as they transition from adolescence to adulthood. Their awareness of the emotions they experience, their openness toward others, their tendency to have crisis periods regarding their careers in their early 20s, and the underdevelopment of important coping skills are likely to occur. Without intervention, Generation Y may become lost in the sea of their emotions and affinity to go back and forth between various career paths and/or companies trying the find their way. They will tell you how they feel about it, but will have difficulty explaining to you what they should do about it. Because hiring, training, and engagement is costly to an organization, addressing the strengths and challenges of Generation Y's psychological awareness will be imperative.

No-brainer coaching solutions

CS1: Understand real problems, but don't accept excuses

Although this coaching solution is a no-brainer, it is an important reminder to help you decrease your frustration with this generation. There is a significant difference between describing a real difficulty/problem and offering an excuse to get out of trouble or an undesirable task. If you hear an inappropriate excuse, don't allow it. Set the culture of your organization to be one that is intolerant of pathetic excuses. Once you set this standard, people start becoming hesitant of breaking the cultural norm. If an excuse smells like crap and looks like crap, then it is crap. Period. Don't allow it.

If excuses continue or if you are starting to see real difficulties and distress, recommend that your Gen Y employee contact the company's Employee Assistance Program (EAP) for a few psychotherapy sessions to help them better understand their thoughts, feelings, and behaviors that are causing distress.

Why it works

This coaching solution is a valuable one, because it fosters a culture of honesty and openness. It is important that we feel supported when life becomes stressful, but it is also important that we are held accountable and to the same standard as other employees. If a workplace community is created where excuses are tolerated without accountability then they will simply increase, and productivity will decrease. It is important to be empathetic, not gullible.

CS2: Emotional dissection

In the workplace, it is hard enough to deal with different personalities and problems. Throw on top of that heightened emotional awareness and difficulty coping, and a supervisor is bound to become overwhelmed and frustrated. We recommend a very simple and important coaching solution pulled from the tool bags of therapists: Help your Gen Y employee understand what is real and what is not. What do we mean by that? Do not be afraid to challenge your Gen Y employee about their emotions. No, we do not mean question whether they are feeling sad or not. What we mean is challenge them when you feel they are having an inappropriate response to a suggestion you offered. Also challenge them when they blame their lack of performance on an issue that you perceive is not a good enough reason for poor performance. To do this, ask them the following:

> What are you feeling?
> What are you thinking?
> What happened before you thought and felt that way?
> Are there other reasons that you may be feeling or thinking a certain way?
> If this happened to your friend and they told you about it, what advice would you give them?

This emotion dissection is a very important skill and a crucial quality to develop in the workplace. It increases self-control, which is a very important quality with regard to leadership. In addition, it enhances reality testing, a skill that is often underdeveloped in this population. Of course, if you feel your Gen Y employee is consistently having problems with this, you may want to refer them to a therapist (if the problem seems emotionally or psychologically based).

Why it works

This coaching solution helps Generation Y with reality testing and self-control by differentiating between actual problems and problems that are more personal, subjective, or emotional in nature. It also helps them develop their ability to cope with their emotions and reactions, and see the bigger picture. Helping them understand their possibly irrational responses and feelings regarding a situation will only help them manage their emotions better and hone their leadership abilities. It will also help them develop accountability for their emotional responses and experiences.

CS3: Chunking information

With an overload of information, attention spans seem to be shorter today. Therefore, to reach Generation Y, short blurbs of information are more effective than long-winded instructions or multiple details. This is probably the result of their preference for multitasking and engaging in multiple forms of stimulation at the same time. If one has information coming from all directions, it is easier to handle input in short blurbs then to try to take it all in for each task. We are definitely not suggesting that you offer step-by-step instructions, but rather offer direct and concise instructions, along with direct and concise expectations. When possible, chunk information and tasks together, so that it can be digested better. This tactic will also be helpful for those employees that have attention deficit problems.

Shrinkwrapped

Chunking is a technique used to enhance memorization when the information can be divided into small and easy to remember chunks. For example, it's easier to remember (405) 321-8953 then it is to remember 4053218953. The more the information can be placed into meaningful chunks the better the memorization and the easier it will be to recall.

Why it works

Because the capacity of our short-term memory ranges from five to seven items, chunking information into "bite-size" groups increases our ability to retain information into our long-term memories. Generation Y's predilection for multi-tasking has resulted in a preference and, for most, a learned style of accepting information most successfully through small chunks of information.

Brainer coaching solutions

CS4: Teachable moments: Tell me, and I may not listen. Help me understand, and I will

Generation Y is apt to ask for advice or guidance, often more frequently than their bosses can tolerate. Although it may be easier to just tell them what to do, this is not always easy, because advice to Generation Y needs to be offered in a careful and tactful way. Although they are more willing to ask questions, they are also less open to being told what to do. Telling Gen Y what to do will only shut down their ability to listen and bring defenses up. However, answering a Gen Y's questions and helping them think through their own solutions will likely have positive benefits. Using this "teachable moments" approach will help Gen Y come up with their own answers in the future, but first they need your help to teach them how.

You will know that you are facing a teachable moment when you simply want to tell Gen Y what they did incorrectly and how to fix it. It may be helpful when confronted with a stressful situation to take a moment (even if through gritted teeth) and remind yourself that this could be a teachable moment that will benefit each party involved and the company as well. Some suggestions to help your Gen Y employees understand the problem at hand are:

> ‣ Ask inquisitive questions to get more details, and assist them in exploring the problem with you.

> Stay focused on the problem instead of seeking blame for why the problem occurred.

> Put the problem in perspective and try not to be so serious. If the world is not ending and no one's life is in danger, then time can be taken, even if not immediately, to dissect the issue.

After some time assisting your Gen Y's with a problem you can encourage them to think of it on their own and then meet with them at a later date to discuss their conclusions and strategies. You are assisting your Gen Y to internalize their problem-solving process and seek guidance within themselves rather than wasting your valuable time on what may be a problem of minor importance.

Why it works

Teachable moments may take time in the beginning. But, by helping your Gen Ys internalize these skills, less time will be wasted in the future. Help them develop better problem-solving skills and increased reflection instead of immediate reaction. The alternative to teachable moments is answering the same questions, and having to deal with the same problems, over and over again. We can see a problem as an annoyance and something to be quickly fixed (over and over again), or we can slow down and view the problem as something with greater importance, a teachable moment.

Idea into action

A manager we spoke with talked about how annoying it was and what a time waster it was to be faced with the same problems repeatedly by the same employees. He expressed that he felt like a broken record, offering the same advice and guidance. He was extremely frustrated over the lack of independence certain employees demonstrated with regard to problem-solving. We asked him to try the teachable moment approach. Rather than just telling them what to do, he sat down with one or two of his employees and problem-solved with them. He provided them with some space to come up with their own solutions rather than guiding them through the process. He asked them questions to get to the root of the problem, so they would be able to think more analytically and independently about potential solutions. Although this approach took some time, he was impressed with his employees' ability to start internalizing his teachable moments, enhancing their own problem-solving skills.

Big-brainer coaching solutions

CS5: Turn annoying problem behaviors into opportunities to increase coping mechanisms

If you have ever become frustrated with a Gen Y worker and felt that you have lost your cool, we want you to know that you are not alone (that's why we wrote this book). Like physical inertia, it is human nature to continue to respond and act in the same way we always have. Frustration occurs when nothing changes. Yet, we keep engaging in the same behaviors and wonder why nothing ever changes. We learned during our training as psychologists that psychosis is when one continues to do the same thing over and over again, expecting different results. So, instead of getting frustrated, try our recommended trial and error approach to turn annoying problem behaviors into opportunities for building coping skills.

Generation Y will be able to tell you how they are feeling. But their explanation prematurely stops there. So help them expand their explanations and develop action steps. When your Gen Y worker states their frustration, and this stress is interfering with their performance, assist them with breaking down their problem into smaller pieces. Rather than becoming paralyzed by the overwhelming nature of a challenge, chunk it into manageable tasks. The learning curve with this solution is rapid, so after helping your Gen Y master these skills, you can then offer verbal reminders to reinforce the learned coping skills. It may be beneficial to have your Gen Y employee take notes so that they can refer back to them at a later date when they are again experiencing paralyzing stress. Here are a few suggestions:

> ‣ Remind your Gen Y employee that they can either change the situation or change the way that they react to the situation.

> ‣ Because you have expansive knowledge on how your company works, help them understand what they have control over, and what they can not change in their work environment.

> ‣ Assist them with reframing the problem situation: When stressful events occur we rarely see them clearly. It is difficult to see the positive within a stressful situation. Help them see what they can possibly learn from the present challenge.

> ‣ Help your employees start a stress log which they write down what happened, how they felt, how they behaved, and what they did to cope with the situation. Also have them identify if their

coping mechanism was successful. This will help them start distinguishing between effective and ineffective coping mechanisms that they employ.

Shrinkwrapped

Reframing is a term that basically describes looking at a situation in a more positive light, without losing the fundamental meaning of the problem. One way to notice thoughts that need to be reframed is when you hear words such as: never, always, should, *and* must.

Why it works

Because this may take some time in the beginning, the value of this coaching solution is having your Gen Y employee see situations that occur at work more clearly and understanding what they have control over. It also helps them be more proactive, rather than reactive, about challenges and developing effective coping mechanisms. An added benefit is that the less negative energy and stress that Gen Y generates, the more peaceful your work environment will be.

CS6: Small accommodations go a long way

If an employee has a psychiatric disorder, they are protected by the Americans with Disabilities Act (ADA) stating that individuals with a diagnosable psychiatric disorder (ADD/ADHD and depression are included on this list) cannot be discriminated against. If someone comes to you and has a documented psychiatric disorder, refer to your company's policy related to ADA. However, below we provide some basic suggestions, pulled from the toolboxes of psychologists that can help with performance and productivity for any employee who many be showing attention or mood problems at work.

For ADD/ADHD, we suggest the following accommodations:

> Individuals with ADD/ADHD learn better when the examples are based on real-life situations as opposed to abstract hypothetical situations.

> Write down information and expectations after they are verbalized, so that the individual can refer back to them.

> Allow employees to digitally record important information that is spoken so they can refer back to the tape if they forget the information.

> Break tasks into smaller parts with a clear time of expected completion.

› Offer flexible work hours. (We are not suggesting that you decrease the time at work, but rather offer a flexible schedule where the individual can take breaks with the expectation that the person will make up the time.)

› Create and provide work areas where distractions are reduced.

For depressive disorders, we suggest the following accommodations:

› If an employee confides in you that they suffer from depression, ask if you can assist them by expressing any concern you may have in the future if you notice a change in their mood or work performance.

› Recognize that the changes you observe in your employee's work performance and mood are time-limited and help link your employee to your company's EAP.

› Ensure that educational information regarding depression and other mental health conditions are present in the workplace.

› Offer space that has sufficient light and ventilation.

Why it works

Some psychological disabilities are covered under the American Disabilities Act, so it is not only important that as a supervisor you know how to accommodate individuals with such challenges, it is mandatory. However, throughout the course of one's career, problems may occur that make it difficult to focus or be productive. Making small changes will result in a major advantages for both the employee and the company.

Coaching solutions simplified

Coaching Solution 1

Title: Understand real problems, but DON'T accept excuses.

Purpose: To hold Gen Y accountable by being understanding of real difficulties, but not allowing empty excuses.

Outcome: Fosters accountability, boundary setting, expectation setting.

Coaching Solution 2

Title: Emotional dissection.

Purpose: To help Gen Y develop self-control, good reality testing, and increased emotional management.

Outcome: More realistic perceptions, enhanced coping skills, and improved emotional management.

Coaching Solution 3

Title: Chunking information.

Purpose: To increase your Gen Y's ability to process information by presenting it in small chunks.

Outcome: Higher retention of information, improved task organization.

Coaching Solution 4

Title: Teachable moments: Tell me, and I may not listen. Help me understand, and I will.

Purpose: To increase Gen Y's independence by placing problems in perspective and assisting them in developing and internalizing problem-solving skills.

Outcome: Enhanced independent problem-solving skills, increased self-reflection.

Coaching Solution 5

Title: Turn annoying problem behaviors into opportunities to increase coping mechanisms.

Purpose: To help Gen Ys gain perspective about their work-related problems and reframe issues to make them more manageable.

Outcome: Increased sense of self-control, increased problem-solving skills, enhanced coping skills, increased ability to more accurately reframe situations, and improved stress management.

Coaching Solution 6

Title: Small accommodations go a long way.

Purpose: To adjust the work environment to help employees who may be having mood related or attention related difficulties.

Outcome: Provide accommodations for those in need.

——Chapter 9——

Politics and Gen Y:
Playing the Game Versus
Choosing Not to Play the Game

"Respect mah authoritah!"

—Eric Cartman, *South Park*

Elizabeth Bradley, a human resource manager at a financial services company, relayed the following story: "I have almost 15 years of HR experience and I have generally good relationships with the younger members of my team. One of the managers at a nearby branch, Joyce, asked me to talk to her HR coordinator, Madison, a 24 year old who is new to the company and new to the field. She wanted me to talk with Madison because she was having trouble motivating her. A couple of months after working more closely with Madison, I assigned her to a project that I was leading along with some other members of my team. I delegated all of the responsibilities to the team and told them to send their parts of the project back in one week. After the week was up, I received the information I needed from each team member except for Madison. So I contacted her and asked her where her research was. Madison told me that, 'She didn't get around to doing it yet.' I begrudgingly gave her two more days. Two days passed and I asked her for her research and she told me that the HR director, my boss, told her that she didn't have to complete the work. Evidently she went right over my head and talked to my boss telling him that the project she was supposed to do was 'unnecessary' and 'a waste of time.' I was furious, so I waited a day and then called my boss to discuss the project and the importance of Madison

> *completing her assigned work. My boss conceded that he was wrong and told Madison she had to do it. I just still can't believe that she went over my head instead of voicing her opinion to me. Who does that?"*

Gen Y is not concerned about politics...office politics that is. They speak their minds, demand information quickly, and are not interested in traditional communication channels and etiquette to get their points and opinions across. The idea of superiors has become passé in Gen Y language and has been replaced with "equals." It is not that they are not respectful or capable of playing the "game," it's just that they have no interest in wasting their time schmoozing in order to get some place or complete a task. They see this type of behavior as a Boomer phenomenon that feels conservative and superficial. Although this upfront approach can be refreshing, the corporate culture has not yet shifted away from the corporate ladder, respect for authority, hierarchical chain of command, and so on. This traditional approach is one of "chutes and ladders" where you can fall down a chute as quickly as you can climb up a ladder, but the approach mandates that the hierarchy is inherent and necessary to run a good business. Gen Y on the other hand prefers, and expects, a workplace where lateral communication, regardless of position, takes place. They expect that promotion and recognition will be given based on talent.

Understanding Gen Y's approach to office politics will be imperative in order to help lead them toward success in the workplace. They are the generation that will shape the future of business and define the enduring culture as the Boomers retire. This generation has a solid base on which to set the stage for the future. They are socially conscious, intelligent, value social diversity, embrace difference and change well, and have a "we are family" orientation toward their colleagues. These characteristics are great building blocks when reinforced with excellent, patient mentorship and coaching. Chances of defining and shaping a positive new culture for the future of organizations are boundless.

Back to the (psychological) basics

Every generation has grown up with their own unique cultural zeitgeist. Different environmental, political, technological, scientific, and medical advances and changes have influenced how people understand and know their place in the world. The Internet has propelled the acquisition of information and e-mail has impacted the speed at which communication occurs.

Technology throughout the last 20 years has changed drastically. This technology has always been a way of life for Generation Y. Having rapid, limitless communication methods and instant access to information created a set of expectations and a way of functioning different from other generations who were not raised with these resources at their fingertips. Similar to learning a second language, it is much easier to incorporate the intricacies of a new language into your verbal repertoire at a young age then it is to learn a second language when you are older.

These resources and experiences have influenced the values, morals, and functioning of Generation Y. This has had great impact on their development and expectations with regard to how they interact, how they engage, and how they perform—all core components of workplace politics. The environmental, political, and social issues, and technological, scientific, and medical advancements that have paralleled this generation have uniquely shaped their expectations, values, and beliefs. Walking through metal detectors when you're going to your sixth grade class undoubtedly has an impact on your understanding of your world. Although Generation Y was born in a financially secure time, they will probably be the first generation unable to financially surpass the preceding generation because of issues such as inflation, debt, outsourcing of services, and so on. Additionally, they are beginning their careers with several crises influencing their lives and the workplace, such as arguably the world's largest financial crisis since the great depression, several perpetual wars, a healthcare crisis, political upheaval, and an environmental crisis. Where the Xers experienced the Challenger spacecraft exploding during their formative years, the Y's experienced a terroristic attack of planes crashing into the World Trade Center and the Pentagon. Whereas Veterans experienced solid, developing companies during their careers, Gen Y has entered their careers with what seems like a chronic case of corporate scandal and corruption. Again, this undeniably shapes one's perception of the world and their fundamental beliefs about basic issues of safety and trust. This is important to understand, because each of our fundamental values and beliefs shape how we relate to people, what work we choose to do, and what missions and social causes we engage in.

This generation is one of the first to care more about the missions and actions of organizations (for example, environmental policies and social policies) than previous generations when choosing a place to work, or a product to purchase. According to Justin Foster, founder/partner of Tricycle-Brand Development, "From a branding and marketing perspective-the self image of this generation has evolved into a fierce individualism. They identify with certain brands but only as it reflects their values (for example, Apple, Padagonia, and other branded environmentally friendly organizations). It is virtually impossible to reach this generation without emotion. For this generation, word of mouth (especially social word of mouth) is critical." Traditional marketing outreach is no longer effective for this generation. A great commercial is not going to motivate a Gen Yer to buy the latest and greatest. However, buzz on Twitter about a new product, where a portion of the proceeds goes to help the homeless, and whose products are produced in a factory that promotes fair and equal employment practices and environmentally safe production, will likely inspire the purchase. If this much thought goes into purchasing a product, how much thought and decision-making power will be put into choosing a company to work for, or in choosing to remain loyal to a company?

Generation Y's socially conscious and civic minded approach to life has also contributed to their strong push toward working for organizations that share the value of volunteerism. In fact, they are more involved in volunteerism than any other generation before. Due to their social conscience and work-life integration, this generation demands the reshaping of corporate culture to include their values. Their cognitions are clear and defined about the importance of incorporating good and socially conscious business practices, and, if challenged, they will easily job hop without looking back.

People are living and working longer, and there are now four generations colliding together at work (Veterans, Boomers, X, and Y). Even though each person has unique values and beliefs shaped by individual experiences, there are also four generational sets of values and beliefs at play in the workplace. We are seeing the synergies and clashes of the four generations. Although the Boomers and Veterans who shaped the corporate culture were raised to show respect for authority figures based on their title and position, Y's (and many X's) were raised to speak their minds, no matter what and no matter to whom. The values and beliefs instilled in childhood, the generational culture demonstrated in school, and the systems involved in all of our upbringings, directly impact behavior and thought in the workplace.

How the game is played:
traditional politics versus Generation Y politics

Traditional	Gen Y
Follow the rules no matter what.	*Follow rules that work and make your own rules if they do not work.*
The boss deserves respect because if his or her title.	*Equality and give respect only when earned.*
Communicate with respect to someone's position.	*Lateral communication, speak to everyone the same.*
Seniority and talent = promotion.	*Talent, not time = promotion.*
Dress for success.	*Dress for individual style.*
Willingness to start at the bottom and work to the top.	*Wants to start at a top position and finds it difficult to "waste" their talent at an entry-level position.*
Some activity in social causes.	*Activity in social causes very important.*

Advantages of not playing old-school office politics

"Although the connections are not always obvious, personal change is insepa-rable from social and political change."

—Harriet Lerner (1944–), psychologist and author

A leader says:

"They don't play the game. That's why there's no BS or cliques. They have no interest in corporate style politics. It's about action. We need to manage to each individual rather than manage with a general style."
Kent Lewis, president,
Anvil Media, Inc.

They speak up, tell it like it is, and don't like being told what to do

Gen Y typically does not see a distinction of hierarchy within their companies. Of course they know who their CEO is, but they believe that their CEO would like to hear how they feel and what they think. In fact, when it comes to the communication of ideas, they typically espouse a lateral philosophy. Title should not matter, only the quality of the idea whether that comes from the janitor or the VP. This is a strength, because Gen Y, as a group, has very little fear of communication and tends to state what they are thinking. This can result in novel ideas that can propel a project and/or company further. They often want to find their own way of getting to the solution. They are, in many cases, creative and outside of the box thinkers. They might not necessarily appreciate a step-by-step action plan of how to get from point A to B, because they may come up with a better solution by visiting point C and D first. Also, when a decision is made that they have not been privy to, they are known to follow up with repeated questions of "why." Answers of, "This is the way we do it, this is the way it's always been done," are not acceptable and they refuse to play the game of "right or wrong, do what the boss says." This is a very different way of approaching the corporate environment.

Although it is not always appropriate to blurt out your thoughts and feelings, there might be several great ideas locked away in people's minds because they are afraid of the consequences of speaking up and speaking out. Other generations tend to be guilty of closeting their ideas because of their ingrained office "ideologies" that define their way of behaving in the workplace (for example, ideas should be shared in a formalized, structured manner; there is a hierarchy in the workplace that should be respected). This generation is certainly not guilty of biting their tongue or waiting for the "appropriate" time or position. This just may result in amazing advancements, fresh ideas, and wonderful contributions.

So what if you're the vice president? You still need to earn my respect

Generation Y does not give respect simply because someone is their superior. In the Boomer and Veteran work culture, a superior at work could always yell, scream, and be disrespectful with no direct consequences from their employees. What has always been expected is that their employees continue to respect them. Maybe Gen Y is on to something here. In reality, it is not okay to be disrespectful simply because you are the boss. In fact, being respectful and conscientious are qualities that contribute to effective and quality leadership. Generation Y is changing what is and what is not tolerated. They are respectful of people who are respectful to them, regardless of that person's title. Also, once that respect is earned, it provides a solid foundation for a relationship to develop, which is a core component to retaining and engaging Gen Y employees.

For the greater good

Generation Y has civic-minded values and has a commitment to social missions. When organizations listen and respond to their Gen Y employees' values and expectations, which in many cases are positive and beneficial to larger social causes, they are better able to retain and engage this talented generation. You can help develop this generation's leadership skills by helping them engage in activities that are important for the greater good. Further, in this day and age, with environmental, political, social, and economic devastation, this is an amazing opportunity for companies to become more socially conscious and generous, impacting a larger social movement toward better business practices that contribute to the greater good, globally (and it does not hurt your reputation as a company either). Many organizations are already on board, such as IBM and Deloitte & Touche USA.

A leader says:

"In my past job, I managed a mixed generation team who was responsible for different projects. I learned quickly that my Gen Ys were much more engaged and excited about the projects that benefitted the community than the team members from other generations. It's not that the other generations didn't care; it's just that the Ys got really pumped for these kinds of projects."
Emily Scherberth, owner and chief connections officer,
Symphony PR & Marketing

The challenges of not playing old-school office politics

"Would I ever leave this company? Look, I'm all about loyalty. In fact, I feel like part of what I'm being paid for here is my loyalty. But if there were somewhere else that valued loyalty more highly, I'm going wherever they value loyalty the most."

—Dwight Schrute, *The Office*

What's a corporate ladder?

As discussed in previous chapters, this generation has grown up with the sense that they can be and do anything they put their minds to. The self-inflation movement has not only created a generation that has high (and sometimes delusional) aspirations, but also a generation that is prone to a sense of entitlement. They expect that opportunities will be showered upon them, regardless of traditional approaches in corporations requiring hard work through the ranks for better opportunities to be offered. So the common comments such as, "But I'm ready for the open supervisor position," are often met with surprise and annoyance by their bosses who feel that it takes time to hone the skills necessary for advancement/promotion and increased responsibility.

Generation Y does not think that the amount of years spent within their career, much less with the same company, should determine a promotion. It is skill that matters, not the time on the job. The problem is, when you feel entitled to certain opportunities, you are psychologically less connected to or attached to the responsibility that is inherent in the opportunity. For example, if you earn a promotion because you have worked hard, a sense of pride comes with your accomplishment and along with that a sense of responsibility to perform optimally. However, not getting the demanded promotion often leaves a Gen Y feeling like they are not being valued for their full potential when it is clear to those currently in leadership that they are simply not ready yet.

A Gen Y says:

"I manage a group of Gen Y's in a software development and Website design company I work for. I'm a Gen Y myself, but I have to say, we can be a very demanding, high-expectation group. I am constantly being asked about promotion opportunities, but in a way that implies that they deserve the promotion or that the promotion is expected. In fact, a few weeks ago, one of my designers, who is relatively new to the company, sent me an e-mail telling me that he thinks he would be a good fit for the assistant art director position in the firm, and proceeded to list all of the work he has done for the company in the last three months. The funny thing is, he's only worked for the company for three months."

J.D. Haldin, art director,
Software Development and Web Design Company

Data entry, filing, answering the phone...are you kidding me?

With Gen Y's beliefs that they should already be working in positions of leadership, they are often easily bored with their entry-level positions, feeling that it is well below their capabilities. Similar to feeling like they should be running the company after being on the job for a year as previously stated, they often complain of being undervalued when they are asked to learn the ropes and build a foundation and knowledge base that often comes from doing more menial tasks or entry-level jobs. It is hard to buy into the idea of career development and progressive skill-building when you have always been told you are at the top, even before you start working toward the top. A negative consequence with this in the workplace is that when you feel undervalued because you are being asked to engage in tasks that you feel are below you, it can lead to harbored negative feelings and dissatisfaction with your jobs.

A leader says:

"So many of these young people feel they are above the basic things. They feel they should be going on business trips, creating presentations, or pitching on day one. Their sense of entitlement is something I've never seen before. To this day, I still do the grunt work when needed, but they feel they are above that and aren't willing to get their hands dirty. It's shocking to see how they don't want to work hard. I have to remind them that they actually have a job with benefits; however, they'll come back at me and complain that they don't have dental or vision. It's a no win!"
Claudia Ross, owner,
Cross Marketing

Breaks in the chain of command

Generation Y is more likely to disregard the chain of command at their company and speak directly to the person who is in charge of the project they are working on or who they believe will be able to assist them best. Gen Ys believe that they might not need to talk to their direct supervisor when it's actually their supervisor's supervisor who has the answer or approval that they need. But there exists a chain of command within a company for a reason. Breaking the chain of command has lead to an imbalance in the workplace environment and feelings of personal disrespect and lack of respect and honor for the chain of command often result.

A leader says:

"Gen Y walks in on day one thinking that they should be the boss! That being said they view their relationship with their boss more on a peer level, as opposed to mentor to mentee. They are not at all disrespectful, just smart

> *and efficient. So they assume total access, not only to their immediate boss,*
> *but the head person as well."*
> Douglas J. Zogby, CPCU, president
> *Got Game! Consulting*

The takeaways so far...

If you remember nothing else, take away the following:

› Generation Y is not interested in playing old school office politics. They see this type of corporate behavior as an archaic waste of time.

› Each generation's values and beliefs about the workplace stem from their generation's cultural zeitgeist. This generation was exposed to extraordinary political, social, scientific, medical, technological, and environmental advances helping shape the way for the most socially and globally aware and conscious generation. They expect that the values that they hold be reflected in the companies that they choose to work for.

You can use Gen Y's refusal to politick to your advantage by:

- Listening closely when they frequently speak up because great ideas will come, even if you have not asked for it.

- Allowing them to set reasonable relationship boundaries regardless of title, as this develops two emotionally intelligent leadership qualities: respect and desire for workplace interpersonal equality.

- Learning ways to get on board with making your company one that is socially and globally conscious. Not only will this help retain and engage your Gen Y employees, it will make your company more desirable in the marketplace.

When it comes to refusing to play the game, watch out for Gen Y's tendency to:

- Expect to get promoted prematurely.

- Refuse to do, or get bored with, engagement in tasks that they may find menial, even though these tasks are part of skill-building and ultimately help with the advancement and knowledge they desire.

- Be ruthless (and indifferent about the impact it has organizationally) about getting what they want, even if it means going beyond direct leadership.

Now it's time to take some action. Here are the coaching solutions that we recommend to enhance the positives and manage the negatives when it comes to Gen Y and corporate politics.

Coaching solutions: building on strengths and addressing the challenge

It is clear that the corporate environment is already established and the politics that go hand-in-hand with the culture are entrenched. However, as leaders, your goals often include leaving a legacy in the hands of capable, talented individuals. Gen Y is talented and they are capable, but they play by a completely different set of values and standards and, therefore, rules. Rather than forcing them to play the same old game, try understanding this generations' values and standards, because incorporating them into the traditional culture will only help, not hinder, your legacy and their success.

No-brainer coaching solutions

CS1: A shared company vision replaces micromanaging

Like most people, Gen Y does not like to be told what to do. However, as a generation, they are used to soaking up information like sponges because of their constant exposure to new, innovative products; technology; and rapidly changing environments. They are also open to hearing ideas, visions, and goals, as long as these are shared openly versus action plans on how to accomplish these goals and the vision. Understanding this knowledge about your Gen Y employees will assist you with keeping them working for you rather than against you.

More specifically, we recommend sharing your ideas, goals, and vision with your Gen Y employees, but once you have, let them figure out their own way to get there. Of course this cannot be the case in all situations, because certain projects require clear and structured steps. However, whenever possible, let your Gen Y employee have a task with a defined goal and let them complete it in their own way. Watch and see what happens—you may be surprised. In a nutshell, move away from micromanaging your Gen Y employees, as they will not respond well to it. In fact, they may run screaming from your organization faster than you can blink.

Why it works

This strategy works because you are working within the philosophy of this generation rather than against it. Of course this is not always effective and should be used with discretion depending on the project; however, we have been amazed by the effectiveness of this solution once seasoned managers let go a little and show faith in the abilities of their Gen Y employees. Rather than fighting the generational push or continuing the tug of war, cut some slack, let go, and take a chance.

Idea into action

Scott Dodson, COO of Divide By Zero Games, Inc., who works primarily with talented and creative Gen Y staff indicated that the major points of frustration that he has experienced is when he has shared a specific vision of what he wanted with steps on how to accomplish that vision and did not get the positive response he had envisioned from his Gen Y employees. He states that he learned quickly that if he let go of his overarching vision, shared his ultimate goals and what he was trying to accomplish, and then stepped back, his Gen Y employees excelled and exceeded his expectations. He shared that his Gen Y employees are fundamentally motivated to do it the way they want to do it anyway, so providing them with his own ideas of how to get there is usually just wasted breath.

CS2: Clearly define the chain of command

Although this one is a no-brainer, it's one that tends to be put in place reactively, with anger, rather than proactively. We all know that Gen Y tends to disregard the chain of command, often disrupting the corporate vibe. If this is the case, then establish ground rules. Make the chain of command well known if it matters to you and your organization, and make your expectations of following the chain of command clear. If a breach occurs, have a face-to-face conversation clearly delineating what that breach caused, and help them problem-solve how they could have gone about getting their question answered in a way that respected the established rules.

Why it works

This is a proactive solution that clearly delineates how things are done in your organization. When your expectations are clear and the chain of command is visible and understandable then it is less likely that infringement will occur.

Brainer coaching solutions

CS3: Freedom of speech and the workplace constitution

Lateral communication and thinking is in, the concept of upper management knows best is out. Allow for every employee (regardless of generation) to have a chance to voice their ideas and thoughts. We are not talking about a free-for-all or anarchy. We are talking about opening up the lines of communication and allowing for idea communication at all levels. Gathering ideas from all levels not only empowers employees, it allows for the communication of a potentially wonderful idea. So many companies have upper management and administration come up with solutions to problems without ever getting input from the people who will actually work with the problem or issue. Instead of having closed-door meetings about solutions, send the message that something is being worked on and create a space on your workplace Intranet that allows for communication of ideas. Post the problem and let the solutions come in. Also allow this technological resource to be a place for people to post ideas. We are sure you will get a few good ones.

Why it works

Yes, we know you have that little box hanging on the wall in the back of the office, collecting dust, labeled "The Recommendation Box." There is dust on it for a reason. Who checks that anyway? Times have changed. Again, technology and community communication is in. Creating a workplace community space on your Intranet (perhaps entitled the "idea blog") allows for freedom of communication and ideas. In addition, public sharing of ideas triggers other ideas. In a way, it creates an ongoing, virtual think tank.

Idea into action

Glenn Reynolds, a team lead at a managed care company said that every time he turns around, the company "think tank" (called lovingly by the staff as the company "waste tank") creates a change in their documentation program accompanied by useless and boring trainings, often followed by reprimands for not following the "new protocol." The frustration from the line staff stems from the fact that these changes are made without forethought and without input from the people that actually use the documentation system. Glenn described a previous company he worked for that had a system in place where all changes were done in a "grassroots" fashion, utilizing the input and recommendations from the line staff to help make improvements in the systems rather than creating obstacles.

Big-brainer coaching solutions

CS4: A socially conscious shift

This generation is extremely active in social causes. Their parents have produced socially conscious hipsters who want to work for companies that honor and share their values. We recommend playing to this altruistic strength by doing one or more of the following:

> Create opportunities for your young workers to take up a cause, in the name of your organization.

> Have a Gen Y lead team develop a corporate charity event.

> If your organization is team-based, challenge the teams to a "volunteer challenge," where each team (if they want to participate) creates a fundraising event or engages in a project requiring team participation. Of course, this should be followed by a "volunteer challenge" celebration where rewards and recognition are given for contributions.

> Partner up with a not-for-profit organization where your organization offers skills based volunteering.

> Offer a certain amount of paid community service hours or a paid community service day. Of course, these benefits are rewarded to those employees who are in good standing with the company.

> Have your Gen Y's integrate a social cause into an existing product or service (such as a credit card that gives 2 percent to an environmental charity).

Not only will this increase organizational commitment by helping integrate their work life with their personal life and values, it will increase exposure for your company. In addition, this type of action is a natural team builder. Creating volunteering opportunities through your organization also provides natural opportunities for employee recognition, a quality highly valued by your Gen Y employees. Finally, volunteering builds leadership skills. Not only is it hip to get involved these days, it is a necessity if you are going to retain your Gen Y's and keep them engaged.

Why this works

Generation Y wants to work for companies that share their values, including their activism in social and global missions. It is pretty common that they will just as likely choose a company to work for based on the values the company espouses versus the position or salary that they offer. Offering these opportunities is a very important tool in the toolbox when it comes to attracting, retaining and engaging the talent of this generation. In fact, according to the 2007 Deloitte Volunteer Impact Survey, conducted by the Opinion Research Corporation (ORC) using a sampling of 1,000 adults between the ages of 18–26, more than 60 percent of individuals surveyed prefer to work for companies that provide volunteer opportunities, while the same survey suggested that only 30 percent of those questioned felt their companies offered compelling volunteering opportunities. This is an important statistic to keep in mind when considering recruitment and engagement strategies for this generation, especially since it is estimated that upwards of 80 percent of this generation volunteers and tends to have expectations that the companies they work for will share similar values.

Coaching solutions simplified

Coaching Solution 1

Title: A shared company vision replaces micromanaging.

Purpose: To provide your Gen Y employees with opportunities to develop their own creative solutions for expected goals.

Outcome: Promotion of creative thinking, enhancing feelings of value and importance, development of initiative and independence.

Coaching Solution 2

Title: Clearly define the chain of command.

Purpose: To act proactively rather than reactively by clearly defining the chain of command.

Outcome: Clarifies communication expectations with regard to the chain of command, boundary setting.

Coaching Solution 3

Title: Freedom of speech and the workplace constitution.

Purpose: To allow ideas to come from employees regardless of position to improve the chances of gathering the best ideas and recommendations.

Outcome: Increased creativity with regard to solutions for old and new problems, comprehensive company involvement in problem-solving.

Coaching Solution 4

Title: A socially conscious shift.

Purpose: To align the company values to reflect the socially conscious values of Gen Y by offering volunteer opportunities through your organization.

Outcome: Improved leadership skills, team building and recruiting, retention and engagement strategy.

──Chapter 10──

The Shoulders of Giants

"If I have seen further, it is by standing on the shoulders of giants."

—Isaac Newton

Janet is consulting with her supervisor Jim about her supervisee Gwen. "I feel frustrated and overwhelmed, Jim. Gwen is talented with so much potential. I want to see her excel in this company and I know she is capable of it, but her Gen Y mentality is getting in the way. She's just so different than I feel I was when I was at her stage of the game. Work was everything to me. I stayed late. I spent time making copies, getting coffee, and taking minutes rather than doing things that I went to school for and found more interesting. I worked on projects that I didn't want to work on. I learned how to work with people I didn't want to work with. I kissed ass and did what I was told. It's simply frustrating to manage her and her expectations sometimes."

Jim sighs, smiles, and looks compassionately at Janet. After taking a long pause he says, "If I have seen further, it is by standing on the shoulders of giants."

Very few of us excel in our careers without our mentors. They are a part of us and the knowledge they share with us becomes part of our work. Those shoulders that you have stood on to see further were shoulders of those who may have challenged, comforted, and/or inspired you. It is your turn to keep the continuous circle of mentorship and leadership strong. Offer your wisdom, experience, and guidance. Be someone that recognizes the power that you have as a manager by understanding how much your wisdom can help the newest generation in the workplace build a solid foundation of skills and hone their potential to successfully become future leaders and contributors. Whether you are aware of it or not you already serve as a mentor indirectly or directly every day by influencing those who work with you and for you. Imagine the power of your influence if you were to choose to mentor consciously.

You are not alone if you have said throughout the past few years, "What's going on with this generation? They are just so different." Generation Y, just like every generation before, brings new challenges and headaches to the workplace and to the process of mentorship. They have walked through office doors everywhere in record numbers sparking concerns and questions from preceding generations. But Gen Y is here to stay, and their presence in workplaces everywhere will only continue to grow stronger as more of them enter the workforce each day. Be conscious of how you feel and what you think as you are listening to your Gen Y's words and actions. Are you feeling frustrated, shocked, and confused wondering where they learned to demand and expect so much? Are you wondering where their mentors are? Look in the mirror. You have a choice. You can either react to this generation with all of the frustration that results from the miscommunications, different styles of work, varying skill sets, differing social preferences, and so on, or be a giant with sturdy shoulders and help mold their way of working. After all, Generation Y is the future and they need your help (whether they think so or not).

It is important to note the difference between mentoring and supervising. Good supervisors and good mentors can be one in the same; however, there can also be a conflict between the two roles. Supervisors and managers, in positions of authority, ultimately have the goal of doing what is in the best interest of the company. Mentors, on the other hand, ultimately have the goal of guiding their mentees toward what is best for individual growth, keeping in mind the goals and interests of the organization. There can be a conflict between what is best for a company and what is best for an employee. Therefore, establishing a mentor-mentee relationship outside of the supervisor-supervisee relationship can be most effective through formal or informal mentoring programs. However, sometimes a supervisor or manager serving as a mentor is appropriate and potential conflicts can be gracefully handled. Whether or not you intend on providing mentorship to your Gen Y employees, reflecting on your supervisory/managerial style is important, so that you can be conscious of how your values, attitudes, and behaviors impact others. For the remainder of the chapter, we will be focusing on how to hone your own mentoring skills to work most effectively with Generation Y, whether you choose to use these skills as a supervisor/manager or a mentor.

From Ancient Greece to the modern business world in a matter of sentences

The concept of mentoring comes from the Greek mythology poet Homer in his story of *The Odyssey*. When Odysseus, King of Ithaca, left to fight in the Trojan War he entrusted his son Telemachus to the goddess Athena who presented herself as an old friend of Odysseus's called Mentor. Mentor's purpose was to care for and teach Telemachus. Although the shoulders that Isaac Newton was referring to were the great thinkers and scientists that preceded him, such as Copernicus and Da Vinci, we feel that the greatest lessons and personal impact comes from the wisdom and influence passed to us by our personal giants. Through time the word *mentor* has come to mean guide, teacher, or trusted counselor. Mentors are an established part of the educational and career process, especially in professions like medicine. We probably do not have to tell you that mentorship programs are becoming increasingly popular in businesses today. Because we learn best through our relationships with others, when a mentoring relationship is strong, the guidance, and interchange is extremely effective for growth and development.

The benefits of mentoring extend not only to the mentee, but also benefit the mentor and the organization as a whole. Mentees benefit from guidance, experience, and expert advice while developing and striving toward personal and professional goals. Mentors often grow and learn through the mentoring relationship, gaining a new knowledge and/or a fresh perspective on different issues. Organizations benefit from mentoring by having a layered monitoring system and by promoting a nurturing work environment created by better relationships among employees throughout the corporate ladder and by the impact it has on productivity, engagement, and retention of younger employees.

We all have our work cut out for us with Generation Y, but we think you are up for the challenge. If you still question whether it is worth your time, consider the 10-60-90 principle, which supports the concept of increased productivity and effectiveness through mentorship:

› When told how to do something 10 percent of what you spent your time saying will be remembered.

› When shown how to do something 60 percent of what you spent your time showing will be remembered.

› When done with the person, 90 percent of what you spent your time doing together will be remembered.

A mentor is usually someone who has been successful in their field, feels confident about their abilities, and wants to share their knowledge and expertise with those who are just beginning on their career journeys. Qualities of an effective mentor are similar to the qualities of an effective leader. It is important that effective mentors and leaders have high emotional intelligence and are on their way (consciously or not) toward self-actualization. Remember Daniel Goleman, the psychologist who popularized and continued work on emotional intelligence? He described the five characteristics of emotional intelligence, which are self-awareness, self-regulation, motivation, empathy, and social skills. Being able to understand the emotions you experience, being in control of how you express your emotions, being motivated toward success, understanding another's point of view, and managing relationships well are qualities one would hope to see in a mentor. Not only are these imperative skills for effective mentoring, they are important skills to help develop in a mentee for optimal professional, as well as personal success. Some qualities of an excellent mentor are:

> Enjoys and can facilitate supportive warm relationships.
> Teaches by example rather than a "do as I say not as I do" style.
> Encourages others.
> Challenges others.
> Shares wisdom.
> Assists with no personal agenda, self-less guidance.
> Strong interpersonal skills.
> Experienced in their fields.
> Knowledge of their company.
> Interested in and enjoys the growth and development of others.
> Can inspire others.
> Interested in seeing their mentees reach higher grounds and levels of success then even they did.

Own your knowledge

We know the influx of this generation into the workplace has been jarring—we have heard your stories. As Generation Y has become a more dominant force in the workplace, you may have worried that previous effective management styles are not working as well. Especially when you started getting strange responses to seemingly innocent feedback, such as tears or an admonishing call from your Gen Y's mom or dad. You have been confronted with bold requests of working from home or working different hours than everyone else or being promoted after the first month of work. This generation, which has brought with them the greatest management challenge ever, is a generation that needs the best mentors possible to combat against the challenges we have described throughout this book and to help them fine-tune their amazing strengths and contributions.

How Generation Y challenges us at work

> Difficulty accepting constructive criticism and feedback.

> Focus on their desired careers at the expense of their current careers.

> Avoid taking responsibility and accountability for mistakes or weaknesses.

> Extreme and unexpected sensitivity regarding perceived failure.

> Demand instant reward and gratification.

> Impatient with the time it takes others to respond to them.

> Preference for digital communication over in-person communication.

> Mixed messages resulting from preferred communication style (that is, informality within digital communication).

> Avoidance of accountability for actions.

> Expectation that companies will adjust to their needs rather than adjusting themselves to meet the needs of companies.

> Loyalty to friends and coworkers, not to the company.

> Value communication with their friends over work responsibilities.

> Share more personal information than you may be ready to hear.

> Use emotional issues/responses to life situations as excuses in the workplace.

> Hold unrealistic expectations and experience dramatic emotional shifts in conjunction with the PQEC.

> Not as observant of others' emotions (bad mood or bad day) as their own and often take others' bad mood or bad day personally.

> Expect to get promoted prematurely.

> Refuse to do, or get bored with, engagement in tasks that they may find menial.

> Are sometimes unknowingly ruthless (and indifferent about the impact it has organizationally) about getting what they want, even if it means going beyond direct leadership.

Are you up for the challenge? To help convince you that Generation Y is worth your time, let's review what strengths they bring with them to the workplace.

The advantages of working with Generation Y

> Confident with a bold belief in their ability to try new things.
> Outspoken so you can ask them what they are thinking rather than making assumptions.
> Jump in without fear, which can result in unexpected success.
> Work well with defined and clear expectations.
> Natural team players.
> Care what respected others think of them.
> Have extraordinary technology communication skills and can create new communication possibilities for your company.
> Have great technology skills and can offer creative, new suggestions to help streamline processes.
> Effective at communicating within multiple mediums simultaneously.
> Have a wide variety of social connections via technological communication.
> Embrace work/life integration.
> Demand work conditions that potentially benefit everyone (such as, flexibility with work time, less formality, improved work relationships, increased access to digital media).
> Immense initiative.
> Enhanced group social abilities and team player attitudes.
> High value for relationships at work.
> Globally and socially conscious, thereby, influencing the companies they work for to be more aware and active.
> Highly developed emotional self-awareness and expression.
> Open to asking for help and guidance.
> Socially inclusive and understanding of those different from them.
> Desire for workplace interpersonal equality among all ranks.
> Value helping others.

Just like previous generations, they are different and unique, and some Gen Y employees will shine while others will not. Many are equipped with the skills to excel and have the potential to illuminate your organization.

Mentoring Gen Y in three easy steps

> *"It always helped me to visualize young people entrusted to my care as 'works in progress.' Instead of seeing the many weak areas of the young (especially with regard to knowledge) I saw them as working through stages, wanting to grow, but needing direction as to how to best do this. There were always your 'stars' that you knew from your first encounter, were extraordinary and would clearly be extraordinary later. However, what always shocked me the most, were the mentees who seemed to be the most challenging and ended up being the ones that grew the most, were most appreciative, and/or distinguished themselves in some extraordinary way down the line. They are kind of like belated gifts that revealed their true selves later, and with more struggle, but were none the less gems. Seeing this throughout the years as a mentor made me a better, kinder, more gentle, and less judgmental of a person. Seeing your mentees as 'works in progress' is a good way to encourage their human potential and achievement. It is also a way to lessen the overwhelming sense of, 'How am I ever going to get them from point A to point Z?' While there are some that for whatever reason can only make the journey from A to G there are others that will go all the way to Z, even when they were the ones you never expected would make it there. It's the mentor's responsibility to help her mentee see her gifts and to facilitate their expression. Even if the initial belief of the mentee is that she doesn't have many/any valuable gifts. We all matter and we all have gifts and we all can contribute to an organization that hires us. The mix of the person's gifts and the organization's true mission are what creates the magic. Of course, there are mismatches but if the organization clearly states and lives their mission and the employee is attracted to the message then there should be some way for mentees to succeed. The key is do we put our money where our mouth is as an organization? Is how we act consistent with what we say we want—for both the mentor and mentee? If not, then the mix is not good and both the mentor and mentee will be challenged to grow or select another organization."*
>
> *M.L. Corbin Sicoli, PhD,*
> *Professor Emeritus of Psychology*

Mentoring Gen Y carries a heavy responsibility. Using your knowledge about this generation and your wisdom from your life experience, you can alter your natural mentoring abilities in order to help pave the way to groom this future generation of leaders and contributors. You have spent a lot of time reading about techniques and solutions for how to address specific challenges, now it is time to think about your overall mentoring style and issues to be aware of when mentoring Gen Y. We offer three steps to contemplate in order to analyze your current mentoring style and hone in on the qualities that will make your mentoring most effective for your youngest employees.

Step 1: Reflective mentoring

What are your thoughts/general feelings about this generation as a whole?

_____

_____

Think about the Gen Y employees that you are currently mentoring or would like to mentor:

How are they different to mentor than other generations?

_____

_____

How do you see your Gen Y employees (as kids, as stars, as difficult, as potential)?

_____

_____

Do you feel that Generation Y has placed expectations on you that you feel need to be modified?

_____

_____

Are there any qualities that you feel you share in common with your Gen Y employee? Any qualities that you feel are very different?

_____

_____

Step 2: Investigate the possibility of biased judgments and stereotypes at work

Looking back at your answers, is it possible that you need to change your perspective about your Gen Y employees? Based on the way they interact with you, do you think that their perspective also needs to be altered for you to be as effective of a mentor as you would like and they may need? If your answer is no to either of those questions, then let us all know where you are working and what planet it is located on. If you are like most, you have realized that Generation Y is unique and that there are specific frustrations and events that have occurred that have lead you to see Generation Y in the particular light that you do. The same goes for Generation Y and how they perceive your presence in their life. Mentoring is not an easy task. Some mentees will let you down. Some will excel. What is the best perspective to have of Generation Y when mentoring them? That is an answer you will have to battle with a bit. But, it is important to battle with your current perspective to make sure that biased judgments and broad generalizations/stereotypes are not shading how you interact with your Gen Y employees. Perhaps you see this entire generation as entitled. Perhaps you see them as unreliable. Perhaps you see this generation as talented and full of potential. Whatever preconceived notions you have, we argue that they can be dangerous when entering into a mentor-mentee relationship because just like every other stereotype or judgment we have with any other group, stereotypes tend to blind and deafen our ability to interact in the present and defeat our ability to truly guide someone effectively.

Shrinkwrapped

Stereotypes are generalized (sometimes accurate, but often overgeneralized and incorrect) beliefs about a group of people. They are often based on an image about what people in that group are like. When we have a stereotype, we tend to look for evidence to support that stereotype, even when it is inaccurate.

To counteract broad generalizations that you may hold about this generation as a whole, which ultimately will reduce your effectiveness as a mentor, we suggest mentoring consciously for the next few weeks by doing the following:

1. Be aware of the thoughts and feelings you have when interacting with your Generation Y employees.

2. Make a conscious note of whether or not you are entering into a discussion with your Gen Y employee with preconceived notions about their responses, reactions, or motivations.

3. Challenge yourself to look for disconfirming evidence that goes against your stereotype, because we are so much more comfortable looking for confirming evidence to support our stereotypes.

4. When you find confirming evidence to support your stereotype, adjust your perspective when dealing with them in that moment ("this is a teachable moment, (blank) is a work in progress...").

Although this task may sound easy, stereotypes are ingrained in most of us and difficult to change. The first step is recognizing that you have them about this generation, just like the Veterans had about the Boomers and the older Xers and the Boomers had/have about the younger Xers, Y's and so on. Once you recognize that you are operating under assumptions that are generalizations, challenging yourself to look at each Gen Y employee as a unique individual with individual strengths and weaknesses, versus a reflection of the whole generation, will hopefully lead to a more balanced perspective. This will ultimately improve your effectiveness as a mentor.

Step 3: Your mentoring toolbox

Once you have challenged your generalizations and tweaked your perspective about Generation Y in a direction that will facilitate your desire to teach and mentor this generation, you will be able to form a useful and productive relationship to help your Gen Y employees become the best they can be. There are two items that we think are essential to have in your toolbox. "The Leveler" (which will balance out the knowledge that you now have about Gen Y with the stereotypes you may have) and "The Hammer" (straight advice to get you started). Add these two tools to your current mentoring toolbox and be sure to always fine tune your attitude for your next mentoring project by reading, reflecting, and learning more about the mentoring process through the many books, trainings, and other materials available about this process.

The Leveler: What to remember about Generation Y when mentoring them:

> Relationships are a top priority.
> Feedback and reassurance is appreciated and motivating.
> Interactive dialogue is valued.
> They want to feel special. Help them personalize their own goals and assist them with getting there.
> They learn by actively doing, not lecturing or listening. Remember the 10-60-90 Principle—do with them for better retention than have them do themselves.
> They want to work on their own terms. Provide structure and expectations and then let them come up with the solutions.
> They value education and training.
> They want to know why something has to be completed or done a certain way. Help them answer their own questions through

Socratic questioning rather than continually having to answer it for them yourself. Make them do the work.

> They have high expectations and lots of demands. Set limits and boundaries in the relationship to help manage demands and expectations.

> There is a tendency toward external motivation. To help internalize motivation, provide praise and reward only when earned.

> Create a collaborative mentoring process.

The Hammer: Keep in mind the following issues when entering into a mentoring relationship:

> Be sure the mentor-mentee relationship feels like a good fit for both parties.

> Commit to an agreed amount (and reasonable amount) of time to work with your mentee.

> Have a conversation at the beginning of the mentoring relationship about what they can expect from the mentoring relationship and what you expect from the mentoring relationship-establish boundaries.

> Co-create goals for the mentoring relationship.

> Be consistent, trustworthy and dependable.

> Act ethical at all times.

> Align your mentoring mission with the mission of the organization and make this known.

> Be a positive role model—walk the walk and talk the talk.

> Maintain confidentiality.

> Advise—do not preach or be a parent.

> Actively listen versus talking all of the time.

> Share your experiences and provide examples.

> Co-create opportunities to share in the learning process.

> Read and learn specifically about mentoring; it's not as easy as it appears.

> Have fun as you are contributing to shaping the future.

With these tools in mind, try to enter the mentoring relationship with a fresh, untarnished perspective. You have the potential to change someone's life and help shape their personal and professional development. Just as you may fondly remember the person that helped shape your career and/or life, you too can serve as "that person" for someone else. Good luck and enjoy the journey.

Epilogue

The Final Takeaway

"In case you're worried about what's going to become of the younger generation, it's going to grow up and start worrying about the younger generation."

—Roger Allen, contemporary American writer

You now know what makes Generation Y tick. You have insight into why they act the way they do, and you understand how to manage their unique strengths and challenges. But times, they are a-changin', rapidly! Even during the months when we wrote this book, our country began experiencing a devastating economic downturn, which led to a bailout that can potentially run into the trillions and we experienced an extraordinary and historic presidential election. Although we have little idea of how this will impact Generation Y, and every other generation that came before or will follow, we could not ignore what is currently happening, as it has and will have a profound impact on all of us. What we know for certain, is that change is the only constant. Therefore, it is important to use these exercises and coaching strategies, but remember, as with any business endeavor, it is important to remain fluid and adapt your strategies to accommodate society's cultural shifts and how they relate to the attitudes and mores of your personnel.

On the horizon

Generation Y grew up during a time of financial security, and along with that security they were encouraged to have big dreams and big plans when it came to career, as well as life. In light of the current economic conditions causing job and financial insecurity for all of us, the clash between Gen Y's expectations versus the reality of the economic catastrophe may cause a monumental crisis of confidence for this generation. In fact, a recent article written by Eve Tahmincioglu from msnbc.com indicates that unemployment rates for workers under 29 (Gen Y) has skyrocketed to 11 percent compared to the overall 7.2 percent as of December 2008. Not only can this be crippling to the grand expectations this generation has as they enter the workforce, panic may set in as they realize their parents, who are also experiencing the sour fruits of the economy, may no longer be able to support them or finance them as they "find their way." Only time will tell, but we do wonder if the changing times will humble this generation's seeming entitlement and expectations, just as every generation before has been humbled by the events of their time.

The crystal ball

Looking to the future, we predict with confidence that the second half of Generation Y, those currently nine to 17 years old, will impact the workplace in a different way than their older generational cohorts. How they will be different is yet to be determined. Their formative years include continued technological growth, more mature and less financially stable parents, and significant global economic, political, social and environmental change, and uncertainty. Although uncertainty and change is true for every generation in their formative years, no generation has had as much access to information and as rapid a delivery system. One thing is for certain; they will cause a few grey hairs on many of their older Gen Y associates when they are old enough to start demanding that the workforce "change" to meet their needs.

References

Andrews, Robert. In *The Concise Columbia Dictionary of Quotations* quote by Robert Frost. New York: Columbia University Press. 326, 1989.

Bell, Chip R. In *Managers as Mentors: Building Partnerships for Learning* quote by Aaron Goldman. San Francisco: Berrett-Koehler Publishers. 166, 1996.

Bettelheim, Bruno and Emmy Sylvester. "Milieu Therapy: Indications and Illustrations." Psychoanalytic Review 36 (1949): 54-68.

Brainyquote.com, s.v. "Lee Iacooca Quotes." *www.brainyquote.com/quotes/authors/l/lee_iacocca_2.html/* (accessed November 13, 2008).

Brill, A.A., trans. *The Basic Writings of Sigmund Freud*, Modern Library Edition. New York: Random House USA, Inc., 1995.

Cameron, Gail. In *Rose: A Biography of Rose Fitzgerald Kennedy* quote by Rose Kennedy. New York: Putnam, 1971.

Castellaneta, Dan. *"Kamp Krusty."* Disc 1, Season 4. *The Simpsons*. DVD. Directed by Baeza, Carlos, David Silverman, Jeffrey Lynch, Jim Reardon, and Mark Kirkland. Los Angeles, Calif.: Columbia 20th Century Fox Television, 1992.

Cline, Foster and Jim Fay. *Parenting Teens with Love and Logic*. Colorado Springs, Colo.: NavPress Publishing, 2006.

Cooperrider, David, Diana Whitney, and Jacqueline Stayros. *Appreciative Inquiry Handbook, Second Edition*. Ohio: Crown Custom Publishing, 2007.

References

Deloitte US. "Deloitte Volunteer Impact Survey (ORC)." Deloitte US, *www.deloitte.com/dtt/cda/doc/content/us_comm_volunteerimpact_survey_results2007(2).pdf* (accessed September 8, 2008).

Erickson, Erik. *Childhood and Society, Second Edition.* New York: W.W. Norton & Company,Inc, 1950.

Fagles, Robert, trans. and Bernard Knox, ed. *The Odyssey.* New York: Penguin, 2006.

Feldman, Daniel. *The Handbook of Emotionally Intelligent Leadership: Inspiring Others to Achieve Results.* Paonia, Colo.: Leadership Performance Solutions, 1999.

Franken, Al. *Stuart Saves His Family.* DVD. Directed by Harold Ramis. Hollywood, Calif.: Paramount Pictures, 1995.

Gandhi, Mahatma. *All Men Are Brothers: Autobiographical Reflections.* New York: Continuum. 108, 1980.

Goleman, Daniel. *Emotional Intelligence: Why It Can Matter More Than IQ.* New York: Bantam Books, 1995.

Gurchiek, Kathy. "Praise Goes Far to Motivate Gen Y." *GBSDirections News letter, January 2008.* 13. www.gallagherbenefits.com/portal/server.pt/gateway/PTARGS_0_24632_555608_0_0_18/January08.pdf (accessed December 18, 2008).

Holdsworth, Claire and David H.J. Morgan. In *Transitions in Context: Leav ing Home, Independence and Adulthood* quote by Haim Ginott. New York: Open University Press. 48, 2005.

Humphrey, James Harry. *Teenagers Will Be Teenagers* quote by Roger Allen. New York: Kroshka Books, 2002.

Janis, Irving L. *Groupthink: Psychological Studies of Policy Decisions and Fiascoes.* Boston: Houghton Mifflin, 1983.

Jung, Carl G., *Modern Man in Search of a Soul.* Translated by Baynes, Cary F. and William Stanley Dell. New York: Harcourt, 1950.

Maggiom, Rosalie, ed. In *The Beacon Book of Quotations by Women* quote by Harriet Lerner. Boston: Beacon Press, 1992.

Maslow, Abraham H. *Motivation and Personality, Third Edition.* New York: Harper Collins Publishers, 1987.

Maury, Jean-Pierre. *Newton: Understanding the Cosmos* quote by Sir Isaac Newton in a letter from Isaac Newton to Robert Hooke February 5, 1676. Fair Hills, N.J.: New Horizons, 1992.

Minter, Robert and Edward Thomas. "Employee Development Through Coaching, Mentoring, and Counseling: A Multidimensional Approach." *Review of Business* 21, 1 (2000): 43.

Mortenson, Kurt. In *Persuasion IQ: The 10 Skills You Need to Get Exactly What You Want* quote by Stephen R. Covey. New York: AMACOM/ American Management Association. 192, 2008.

Pendleton, David, Theo Schofield, and Peter Tate. *The Consultation: An Approach to Learning and Teaching.* Oxford: Oxford University Press, 1984.

Peter, Laurence J. The Peter Principle. Madison, Wisc.: University of Wisconsin Press. 27, 1969.

Prensky, Mark. "Digital Natives, Digital Immigrants." *On the Horizon*, 9, (October 2001).

Quotationsbook.com, s.v. "Quotes by Darrow, Clarence," *http://quotationsbook.com/quote/22359/* (accessed September 26, 2008).

Quotationspage.com, s.v. "Anais Nin," *http://www.quotationspage.com/ quote/27655.html* (accessed January 6, 2009).

Rogers, Carl R. *Client-Centered Therapy: Its Current Practice, Implications, and Theory.* Boston: Houghton Mifflin Company, 1965.

Rotter, Julian B. *Social Learning and Clinical Psychology.* New York: Prentice-Hall, 1954.

Select Minds.com. "Workplace Connections & Their Impact on Retention, Recruiting, and Productivity." *www.selectminds.com/nc/ PollRelease_businesswire.pdf.* (accesseD November 15, 2008).

Skinner, B.F. *About Behaviorism.* New York: Vintage, 1976.

Ringelmann, Max. "Recherches sur les moteurs animés: Travail de l'homme." *Annales de l'Institut National Argonomique*, 2 (1913): 1-40

Tahmincioglu, Eve. "Under 30? Looking for a job? You're not alone unemployment rate well above average for twentysomething workers." MSNBC.com, *www.msnbc.msn.com/id/28663645* (accessed January 16, 2009).

Templeton, John. In *Wisdom from World Religions: Pathways Toward Heaven on Earth* quote by Carl Jung. Philadelphia: Templeton Foundation Press. 172, 2002.

Thinkexist.com, s.v. "Charles de Lint Quotes," *http://thinkexist.com/quotation/ the_problem_with_children_is_that_you_have_to_put/ 201179.html/* (accessed December 4, 2008).

References

Thinkexist.com, s.v. "James Thurber Quotes," *http://thinkexist.com/quotation/l et_us_not_look_back_in_anger-nor_forward_in_fear/210203.html* (accessed January 6, 2009).

U.S. Department of Justice. "Americans with Disabilities Act of 1990." U.S. Department of Justice, *www.ada.gov/pubs/ada.htm* (accessed November 4, 2008).

Wilson, Rainn. *Halloween.* Disc 1, Season 2. *The Office.* DVD. Developed by Greg Daniels. Los Angeles, Calif.: NBC Universal Television Studios, 2005.

Index

Index

——About the——
Authors

Nicole A. Lipkin, PsyD, MBA, is the owner of Equilibria Psychological and Consultation Services, LLC, a group psychology and coaching practice-based in Philadelphia. She coaches and consults with leaders/executives, entre-preneurs, small business, and organizations. She also provides coaching and training services for Generation Y emploees and those who manage them.

April J. Perrymore, PsyD, owns an independent psychological practice. In addition to her psychotherapy work with individuals and couples, she special-izes in working with small business owners and entrepreneurs. Previously, she was an assistant professor of psychology, teaching and advising Generation Y.